D1507792

12 SIMPLE STEPS TO A WINNING MARKETING PLAN

Geraldine A. Larkin

PROBUS PUBLISHING COMPANY
Chicago, Illinois
Cambridge, England

ISBN 1-55738-297-2

Printed in the United States of America

BB

3   4   5   6   7   8   9   0

Table of Contents

Preface   v

Chapter One   Getting Started: Or, Nothing Occurs
                   in a Vacuum   1

Chapter Two   The Situational Analysis—Part I   15

Chapter Three   The Situational Analysis—Part II   29

Chapter Four   What is a Market? Or, Will Anyone Buy
                   This Product?   45

Chapter Five   Defining Your Market: Using Specific Measurements   55

Chapter Six   Tuning Your Market Definition   79

Chapter Seven   Nitty Gritty Research   91

Chapter Eight   Finding Your Customers for Feedback   113

Chapter Nine   The Competition   129

Chapter Ten   Positioning   155

Chapter Eleven   Public Relations   175

Chapter Twelve   Putting It All Together   185

Bibliography   211

Index   213

About the Author   217

PREFACE

The purpose of this book is to help people who don't know much about marketing to learn enough basic concepts to develop a good first draft of a marketing strategy for a company product. It is not a substitute for an ongoing, in-depth primary source analysis of a product's markets, but it's a start, and it beats sitting through marketing classes, for which you may have neither time nor money.

The book grew out of a desperate need, on the part of my clients, for a marketing primer, i.e., something that could explain basic marketing concepts in a straight forward and uncomplicated fashion. That has been my goal.

ACKNOWLEDGEMENTS

There are always many people to thank: my parents, my friends, my clients; some outstanding managers, notably Bill White, president of the C.S. Mott Foundation, Pete Plastrik at the Michigan Department of Commerce, and partners Michael J. Cleland and Cameron Duncan at Deloitte & Touche. Mike and Sandy have made it possible for me to continue to learn and practice marketing on a broad basis, reflecting Deloitte & Touche's ongoing commitment to client-driven services. I want to thank my editor, Peter Kacmarek at Probus Publishing for all of his good work.

Most of all, I want to thank Lisa Pajot, my associate at Deloitte & Touche. Without her help, this book literally would not have been completed.

Geraldine A. Larkin
March 1992

Getting Started:
Or,
Nothing Occurs in a
Vacuum

A Definition of Marketing

What marketing is not:

It is not advertising, although advertising is almost always a part of marketing.

It is not sales, although sales are also a part of marketing.

What marketing is:

Marketing is your strategy for taking your product to market. It is **how** you **find** and then **sell** to your customers. Your goal in marketing should be to satisfy customer wants at a profit. Getting to that profit implies a strategy with four parts:

1. marketing objectives;
2. an analysis of the market (what **is** this animal?) and where it is headed;
3. an action plan; and
4. a budget that lists and prices all the resources needed to accomplish your goals and objectives.

These parts are broken down into twelve steps in this book, starting with a marketing objective and situational analysis and ending with a final marketing action plan.

How I Think About Marketing

First you need to figure out what problem you are solving with your product and how you are going to find the people (customers) who have that problem. Once you find them, you need to convince them that you have the best solution to their problem so that **they will buy your product.**

The most common mistake people make is heading off in too many directions. It is far more important to identify the resources you have to work with and then to focus them on a subset of all your potential customers, expanding your marketing efforts as you build sales success.

The Importance of Context

One of the biggest mistakes most people, even old pros, make in marketing is under-valuing the importance of context. Context is everything in marketing. That's because marketing never works in a vacuum. No one can wake up one morning and successfully go out and start selling a new widget without taking two "contexts" into consideration. The first is the company itself, i.e., your business. Trying to develop a product and marketing plan that does not match the business you are in is equivalent to rolling a boulder up the proverbial mountain. It just won't work. A key to successful marketing is thinking through the business. If you are in an environmental cleanup business, then all of your products and marketing activities need to be consistent with that mission. If you are in the business of selling house notions, don't sell clothes. If you are a motivational speaker, you should not be writing mathematics workbooks for third graders as a part of that business.

The second context is the world outside of your business. The more attentive you are to trends going on around you, the more successful you will be in marketing your product. For example, knowing that most Americans now refer to themselves as "environmentalists" should tell you that it will be important to sell earth-friendly (or at least earth-neutral) products in earth-friendly packaging. Tracking these trends can give you a real competitive advantage. One of Michigan's fastest growing printing companies has just launched an entire new product line of note cards printed on recycled paper. Their main marketing message is that the cards are earth friendly. In the jargon of the marketing industry, watching these trends is called "performing a situational analysis." Chapters Two and Three provide a more detailed descriptions of the type of trends to watch. For now, the important point is to know that there are significant goings-on around you which will have a tremendous impact on your marketing success.

Company Objectives

The first step in developing a marketing strategy is to make sure that you have a clear company objective. Some people think of a company objective as their vision for where they want the company to be at the end of some time period, say three to five years down the road. If the vision is clear enough to picture it in your mind, then you probably have a pretty good objective. This is different from a company mission. A company mission tends to be abstract, while an objective is very specific. The example below shows the difference between the two.

Example

Elderhealth Company's Mission:

To promote health among the elderly.

Elderhealth Company's Objective:

To be the leading provider of exercise classes for persons over the age of 65 by 1995.

This difference is important. Most company missions are too vague for a marketing strategy. In the example, you can see why. You could develop thousands of products and marketing strategies that might promote health among the elderly.

A company objective, on the other hand, is a good start because it gives you a specific framework around which you can build your marketing plan.

The best company objectives have four attributes:

1. They are time constrained so that you know when you expect to accomplish them.

2. They are measurable so that you can tell if you've done what you set out to do.

3. They are broad enough to include all aspects of your business, such as research and development, production, and sales. This is helpful because it gives you guidelines on both the type of new products you might want to develop in the future and the products you want to avoid.

4. They create a picture that is shared generally by everyone in the company.

It is impossible to write a marketing plan for any product until you define who you are as a company. Here are two examples of company objectives.

5

Example

.... By 1994, Company ABC will be a leader in the medical industry relating to heart disease through its development and distribution of state-of-the-art surgical instruments.

.... Day Care, Inc. will be the largest franchiser for weekend child care in the Midwest states of Michigan, Ohio, and Indiana by the year 2000.

Both of these company objectives set time limits, can be measured, are broad enough to include all functions of the business, and create clear pictures of their company leaders' goals.

Exercise 1-1

Write your company objective here, making sure to include the four attributes listed above.

What is your time limit?

_____

_____

_____

What will be your measure of success?

_____

_____

_____

Have you made certain that the objective is broad enough to include all aspects of the business?

_____

_____

_____

_____

_____

What picture comes to mind when you read your objective?

_____

_____

_____

How do you think you will accomplish that objective? (The purpose of this question is simply to get your creative juices flowing and to help you start to focus on marketing and how it fits into your company plan).

_____

_____

_____

What will you do between now and the date in your objective? More creative juices should start flowing here.

_____

_____

One way to check whether you've thought rationally about your company objective is to think through the resources you bring to the table (or will be able to, over time), asking yourself if you have sufficient resources to accomplish the objective you have just defined. If you do not, it is probably a good idea to redefine your company objectives until you have sufficient resources at hand to accomplish them.

What resources do you have right now that will help you accomplish your objectives?

_____

_____

_____

_____

_____

People: How many people can you tap to accomplish your objectives?

_____

_____

_____

_____

_____

Finances: What is your budget? Do you have revenues, or can you borrow sufficient cash to accomplish your objectives?

_____

_____

_____

_____

Machines: Do you need machines to accomplish your objective? If you do, do you have them? If not, do you have access to cash to lease, rent, or purchase them?

_____

_____

_____

_____

_____

_____

_____

_____

_____

Supplies: Do you have the supplies you need to accomplish your objective? If not, do you have sufficient cash to purchase the supplies?

_____

_____

_____

_____

_____

_____

Once you have thought about these questions, you will find that it is an easy task to think about a marketing strategy for a product. Everything that you write in the remainder of this book should be consistent with your company's objective, how you think the objective will be accomplished, and the resources you have at hand. Check back with your company objective as you develop your marketing strategy.

The First Official Step: Your Marketing Objective

A marketing objective is a subset of your company objective. It flows from it in the same way that a production objective or revenue objective or personnel objective would.

All marketing objectives have a specific purpose. Normally, the purpose has at least one of the following five results to be successful. Some marketing objectives do all of these things, some do several, and some do only one:

1. increase awareness of your product;

2. decrease resistance to your product;

3. improve your product's image;

4. impart knowledge about your product; and

5. disclose qualifications about your product.

Example

Listed below are several marketing objectives and what they are trying to do:

Introduce product X to its market successfully by the end of 1990.

Result: Imparts knowledge and increases awareness.

Advertise product Y as the most rugged computer disk for the personal computer student market.

Result: Imparts knowledge, increases awareness, and discloses qualifications.

To gain 10 percent of the market share for no-run pantyhose by 1993.

Result: Decreases resistance and increases awareness.

It is useful to write your marketing objectives twice; once before you analyze the market for your product and then again after you have studied your potential customers. You need to start somewhere; you might as well take a stab at an objective now, to provide you with a framework for thinking about your market. You will find that once you have spent time researching and studying your market you will want to change your objective, even if only to refine it.

Exercise 1-2

Write your marketing objective(s) here:

_____

_____

_____

_____

_____

_____

_____

_____

_____

What are the results of the objective if you are successful?

_____

_____

_____

Will it increase awareness of your product?

_____

_____

_____

Will it decrease resistance to your product?

_____

_____

_____

Will it improve your product's image?

_____

_____

_____

Will it impart knowledge about your product?

_____

_____

_____

Will it disclose qualifications about your product?

_____

_____

_____

If it will not have at least one of these results, you need to go back and rethink your marketing objective until you find one that can do at least one of these things.

After you've read through the book, write your marketing objective(s) again here.

What are the results of the objective if you are successful?

_____

_____

_____

Will it increase awareness of your product?

_____

_____

_____

Will it decrease resistance to your product?

_____

_____

_____

Will it improve your product's image?

_____

_____

_____

Will it impart knowledge about your product?

_____

_____

_____

Will it disclose qualifications about your product?

_____

_____

_____

In the case of a start-up or very young company, your marketing objective may be identical to your company's objective. On the other hand, if this marketing plan is only for one product of many, then what you develop with this book is only a subset of your company's total marketing objective. In this case, you need to go through the whole book for each product line and then pull it together into a master plan.

The Situational Analysis
Part I

D efinition of Situational Analysis

Once you have defined your company objective and taken a stab at marketing objectives, step two in actually developing the specifics of your product's marketing plan is to perform a situational analysis. In other words, you need to know what is surrounding you before you start selling your product. Defining and describing those surroundings and their potential impact on your product is called a "situational" or "environmental" analysis. Word choice depends on the individual. In my experience, they are exactly the same thing.

Basically we all live in four overlapping environments. Each can impact the potential success of your product. They are:

1. your economic environment, including your own industry;

2. your legal environment;

3. your social and cultural environment; and

4. your technological environment.

By considering all four, you will discover where potential opportunities and problems are for your product. Each environment affects your customers' buying behavior. For example, people who live in cold climates buy more heating oil and are probably more sensitive to price differences (because they buy a lot) than people who live in warm climates. If you live in a country where you earn a lot of interest on your savings, you will probably spend less of your income on consumer goods such as books, movies and radios than you would if you lived in a country where you only earn 1 or 2 percent interest on your savings. If companies can borrow money at no or low interest rates for hi-tech machines, they will buy hi-tech machines.

The hard part about analyzing these environments is that the world is always changing. Worse, each of these factors can have an effect on the others. All you can do is try to take a snapshot in time, describing as best you can the different elements as they exist right now and how they may have changed in recent years.

In marketing, what matters most is how each environment will impact your product, either positively or negatively. As you think about each, remember that the key question you need to continue to ask yourself is,

"How does this impact my product and how I plan to market it in this environment?"

The Economic Environment

Your goal in looking at the economic environment of the country where you want to sell your product is to get a sense of its total business climate. For the United States, a review of the indicators listed below should give you a fairly good idea of how the country is doing. To get the indicators' values, you need to track down a copy of *The Business Conditions Digest* published by the U.S. Department of Commerce's Bureau of Economic Analysis. It should be available at any university library. Other sources include *Fortune* magazine, *Business Week* magazine, *The Wall Street Journal*, and various economic indicator reports from banks, investment firms, and accounting practices. Good librarians also will be able to suggest sources. To see trends, look at the numbers for each indicator over the past several years and then at their projections for this year and the next. Are they increasing, decreasing, or staying about the same? Together the indicators will give you a feeling for how the country's economy is holding up these days.

Exercise 2-1

ECONOMIC INDICATORS

Indicator	Increasing/Decreasing	By How Much?
Gross Domestic Product		
Inflation Rate		
Personal Income		
Corporate Profits		
Contracts/New Orders for Plant Equipment		
Unemployment Rate		
Number of New Current Businesses		

Indicator	Increasing/Decreasing	By How Much?
Number of Business Failures		
The Cost of Money		
Other Indicators:		

It also is a good idea to get on the telephone and talk to people such as economists, business editors at the local newspaper, university professors, etc. Verbal information often can be more timely and insightful than written information. To be on the safe side, use both.

CONTACT LISTING

CONTACT _____ DATE _____

ADDRESS _____ PHONE _____

COMMENTS _____

_____

_____

CONTACT _____ DATE _____

ADDRESS _____ PHONE _____

COMMENTS _____

CONTACT _____ DATE _____

ADDRESS _____ PHONE _____

COMMENTS _____

_____

_____

Exercise 2-2

What about your industry? It is also important to review industry trends for your product to get an overview of what is going on over time.

INDUSTRY OVERVIEW

INDUSTRY SIZE:
_____

YOUR MARKET SHARE:
_____

TECHNOLOGY:
_____

INDUSTRY GROWTH:
_____

RECENT CHANGES IN LEADERSHIP:
_____

_____

COMPETITION:
_____

CHANGES IN LEADING PRODUCTS: _____

_____

_____

_____

_____

_____

_____

Use the following pages to list the people you interview regarding industry trends as well as what they have to say.

CONTACT LISTING

CONTACT _____ DATE _____

ADDRESS _____ PHONE _____

COMMENTS _____

_____

_____

_____

CONTACT _____ DATE _____

ADDRESS _____ PHONE _____

COMMENTS _____

_____

_____

_____

CONTACT	DATE
ADDRESS	PHONE

COMMENTS

_____

_____

_____

_____

If you are unfamiliar with your own industry, start asking people who are what is happening. Who do you ask? A university professor familiar with the industry, an editor of one of the industry's trade journals, an industry analyst for an investment firm, potential competitors (for those of you with true courage), sales people in the industry, and yourself on a day when you are feeling particularly brilliant. You probably know more about the industry than you think.

Exercise 2-3

During your discussion, also ask for examples of good predictors of how the industry is doing. Then go check out the trends and forecasts related to these indicators.

What are those predictors? Are they changing? How?

PREDICTION	CHANGES GOING ON
1.	
2.	
3.	
4.	

Many, many organizations collect information regarding the trends in specific industries. Two of the best information sources are the U.S. Department of Commerce's *Business Conditions Digest*, which is published monthly, and Dun and Bradstreet's industry reports. Other research organizations that produce reports include:

Arthur D. Little Co.
17 Acorn Park
Cambridge, MA 02140

Frost and Sullivan
106 Fulton Street
New York, NY 10038

Technology Futures
6034 W. Courtyard Drive
Austin, TX 78730

There are many more research companies to draw from, but catalogs from these three companies should give you a head start. If you do not find pertinent information in anything they provide, call them and ask for referrals.

The Kiplinger Newsletter is another wonderful source of data. Available since 1923, its subscription rates are very reasonable, given the information packed into each issue. For more information write to: The *Kiplinger Washington Letter*, 1729 H Street NW, Washington, D.C. 20006. Telephone: (202) 887-6400.

Before you move on to the legal environment, take some time to look at all the information you have gathered and ask yourself, "what are the implications for me?" You may need to change your product line, sell differently, or come up with new packaging. The main point is that these trends are telling you something, and you need to study them until you figure out what it is. Here's an example: My brother builds houses. As he watched industry trends and economic trends several years ago, he realized that it would be better to build fewer houses because bank lending was drying up, and his target market should no longer be lower income families because they would have harder times getting a mortgage. Instead, his focus needed to be double income professional households. Based on those trends, he changed his focus and did very well.

The Legal Environment

Along with the economic environment, the shape of the country legally and politically also impacts every business. For example, changes in speed limits impact the types of cars we purchase, the types of accessories we want (i.e., radar detectors), the amount and type of gasoline we purchase, and how many activities we can fit into a day.

A special note for potential exporters: If you are planning to do business in a foreign country, **always** review its political stability. Usually, trade associations can help you find out what you need to know. The person to contact is the association's government affairs representative.

If you are planning to sell your product in the United States, it is worth your time and aggravation to contact every state where you plan to sell to discover any regulations that could impact your activities. Be sure to include environmental regulations if you are in manufacturing. Also take time to check with federal government agencies if you are planning to cross state lines, or even if you aren't. They may have licensing restrictions that could affect you.

Exercise 2-4

Start with the federal agencies. To help you get started, some of the more significant agencies are listed below. As you contact the agencies, ask about others that might have regulations with an impact on your business.

✦ The Department of Commerce, which oversees virtually all aspects of business. To find out about its rules and regulations you can write to: 14th Street and Constitutional Avenue N.W., Washington, D.C., 20230. Telephone: (202) 377-3263.

✦ The U.S. Small Business Administration (SBA) is housed within the Department of Commerce. Although the SBA has too many programs to mention here, it should be said that its various mailing lists are worth getting. Contact the SBA at: 1441 L Street N.W., Washington, D.C., 20005. Telephone: (202) 663-6365.

✦ The Environmental Protection Agency oversees water, air, solid waste, hazardous waste, pesticide and food and drug regulations. Write to: Small Business Ombudsman, Environmental Protection Agency, 401 M Street S.W., (A-149C), Washington, D.C. 20460. Telephone: 1-800-368-5888.

✦ The Food and Drug Administration regulates most food, pharma-
ceuticals, and some agricultural products. Write to: 5600 Fishers
Lane, Rockville, MD 20857. Telephone: (301) 443-1544.

✦ The International Trade Administration implements rules of international trade, including both domestic laws related to dumping,
export control and boycotts, and international codes governing
trade and trade restrictive activities. Write to: U.S. Department of
Commerce, International Trade Administration, Washington, D.C.
20230.

✦ The National Bureau of Standards (NBS) develops, maintains, and
disseminates hundreds of measurement standards. NBS is also the
focal point for computer technology activities in the federal government. Write to: NBS Inquiry Service, Administrative Building,
Room A537, National Bureau of Standards, Washington, D.C.
20234. Telephone: (301) 921-2318.

✦ The Patent and Trademark Office examines patent and trademark
applications to determined whether an invention is patentable or
trademark may be registered. Write to: Commissioner of Patents
and Trademarks, Washington D.C. 20231.

List the other agencies you should call here. (If you aren't sure, call
anyway; you never know.)

FEDERAL AGENCIES

AGENCY	ADDRESS	PHONE

Exercise 2-5

List all the regulations that apply to your product, when you requested them, and when they were received:

REGULATIONS

REGULATION	DATE REQUESTED	DATE RECEIVED

Exercise 2-6

The next step is to list the potential impact of each regulation on your product. If there is no impact, you do not need to analyze any of the documents you now have.

IMPACT CHART

REGULATION	IMPACT	PRODUCT CHANGES

Exercise 2-7

Repeat the same process for each state you want to penetrate with your product on the blank page that follows. Every state has its own Department of Commerce or an equivalent organization. If you aren't sure where to start, call the governor's office.

STATE AGENCIES

REGULATION	IMPACT	PRODUCT CHANGES

Exercise 2-8

To be on the safe side, smart marketers take a sample of cities in their sales area and call them about any policies that might impact their product. In particular, you want to get to know the folks at the city hall where your company is headquartered.

CITY REGULATIONS

CITY	CONTACT	DATE	IMPACT	CHANGES REQUIRED

The Situational Analysis Part II

S ocial and Cultural Environment

Step three in your planning process is trying to figure out what is going on around you, both socially and culturally. Much of this is demographics—who we are, what our incomes are, and our ethnic groupings. Simply stated, our cultural environment is made up of our tastes and life-styles. Of all the trends you consider in your marketing plan, socio-economic and cultural trends are often the most critical. The reason for this is that, in the end, we're all selling to people. Whether we are services or manufacturers, people must say yes to us—to purchase or order our product—and we are all most likely to buy from people like us, or people that strike some familiar chord in us. What that means, in marketing, is that it is important to get a strong sense of who we are selling to, what they like, what they don't like, what their values are, etc. The first clues come from a look at social and cultural trends.

As the United States moves through the 1990s, some demographic trends are quite clear:

1. First, we are becoming older and, happily, we seem to be getting healthier at the same time. (The great unknown here is AIDS). According to the U.S. Bureau of Census, 30 million Americans were 65 or older in 1988; some 48 million were 55 or older; and 62 million were 50 or older. These numbers are expected to increase significantly over the next ten years.

2. Most Americans are single longer and more often. People are delaying marriage and children.

3. As of 1990, more than 55 percent of women were in the work force.

4. Childbirth is being delayed, and we are having fewer children. In fact, demographers tell us that without immigration, the United States would have zero population growth today.

5. We are now the sixth largest Spanish speaking country in the world, after Mexico, Spain, Argentina, Columbia, and Peru. The annual after-tax income of the nation's Hispanics, who now number more than 20 million, is approximately $300 billion. At the same time, this group is growing at a rate that is five times greater than the general population. There is actually a much

bigger cultural trend taking place here. In addition to the growth in Hispanics, there is significant growth in the Asian population, largely through immigration.

6. There also has been a huge growth in environmental conscious-ness in the last decade. In a 1990 Louis Harris poll reported by the *New York Times*, 75 percent of us said we would describe our-selves as environmentalists.

7. There also has been a growth in "psychic income." In other words, sociologists are starting to see a trend in people where we increasingly are willing to trade in our incomes and material pos-sessions for meaning in our lives. A sub-trend here is a tremen-dous growth in spirituality. A recent national poll showed that more than 40 percent of Americans listed their relationship to God as the most important thing in their lives.

Exercise 3-1

List here other demographic trends that could impact on your company.

_____

_____

_____

_____

_____

_____

_____

_____

_____

_____

_____

For more information about demographic trends, you might want to read through several issues of John Naisbitt's *The Trend Report* or any of Faith Popcorn's work.

Consumer Tastes

Consumer tastes, which reflect the cultural environment, can be difficult to track because they change rapidly. I spent years watching for a quick and virtually painless method for getting my fingers on the pulse of America's consumers. If you don't have a neighborhood psychic who can help you, the following five day "marathon" has proven to be an excellent and entertaining way to identify present consumer tastes. A friend of mine actually introduced me to the marathon, which I ignored for years until I started teaching marketing and kept coming up against the same problem of identifying consumer tastes. I now swear by this exercise. At first these steps will seem simplistic—until you actually start listing the patterns that emerge from your experience. The pleasure of the process is that it puts your subconscious to work for you, analyzing the trends and patterns your eyes are seeing and ears are hearing.

Exercise 3-2

Step One:

Spend a day in several trendy shopping malls, going into every store. Check out everything. Observe displays, packaging, colors, what people are buying at the counters.

What did you notice?

_____

_____

_____

_____

What patterns did you see?

_____

_____

_____

_____

What colors are dominant?

_____

_____

_____

_____

_____

What are people buying?

_____

_____

_____

_____

Step Two:

Pretend that you are from a different country (even if you aren't) and only have four hours to get the lay of the land. Find a good librarian and ask him or her to give you the best information available that describes the United States. Focus on reference books and business trend issues of major magazines. What did you discover?

What are the main topics of discussion?

_____

_____

_____

_____

What are the issues related to these topics?

_____

_____

_____

_____

What are international trends that could impact you? An example might be the growth of Japanese economic power or the slow down in population growth in India and China.

_____

_____

_____

_____

What are the national trends that could impact you? For example, if most states are in tough shape financially, will that affect you in any way? How?

_____

_____

_____

Step Three:

Go to your favorite magazine store and go through every magazine that strikes your fancy. If you can afford to buy them, do it. If you can't, browse like crazy until the store owner is standing next to you, and then buy several of the most expensive ones to thank him or her for use of the store. What did you notice?

What are people reading about?

_____

_____

_____

Thinking about?

_____

_____

_____

What gets advertised?

What are the values and the tastes that popped up often?

After doing this for several years, I now have some favorite magazines. The reason for each is that they seem to be slightly ahead of the market-place, which gives you a bit of a head start when trying to project where consumer tastes are headed, a critical marketing task. They include:

Architectural Digest: for style and design.

European *Vogue*: for colors, style.

Esquire: for issues of general interest.

Omni: for scientific information.

Utne Reader: for spiritual, baby-boomer trends and topics.

Step Four:

Watch the top ten prime-time television shows back to back for a week, and stay put to see what the commercials reflect. What did you notice?

What are the themes?

What are the types of families?

_____

_____

_____

What do people wear?

_____

_____

_____

_____

What technologies are obvious?

_____

_____

_____

How is color used?

_____

_____

_____

_____

It is important to watch TV, assuming you aren't a television junkie, because the people who develop and produce commercials are paid very well to analyze demographic, cultural and consumer trends, reflecting those findings in their commercials.

Step Five:

Round up copies of the *New York Times*'s top ten best sellers for this week, fiction and non-fiction, and read them, or at least read the first and last chapters so that you can get an idea of what the book is about; or if you are just too swamped, go read reviews of the books. These books are important because opinion leaders read them, and their choice of reading material can give you a lot of clues regarding the state of the American mind. What did you notice?

What are the themes?

_____

_____

_____

_____

What are the types of families?

_____

_____

_____

_____

What do people wear?

_____

_____

_____

_____

What technologies are obvious?

_____

_____

_____

_____

The market plan that you develop will need to be consistent with trends identified, so please take time to check back over this section, in particular, before you finalize your plan.

The Marathon exercise is important for many reasons. It gives you clues to people's tastes and values. It also will tell you what colors and styles are in fashion so that you can integrate them into your product packaging and advertising. And, it will identify key "jargon" words that you might want to integrate into your product description, knowing that they will get your customer's attention and portray your product as timely.

Technological Environment

Technology is changing all around us, impacting each of our markets. Given that 90 percent of all the scientists who ever lived are alive today, you can be sure that technology will continue to change at a faster and faster pace. It is important to stay familiar with the technology related to your product, always thinking about how technological changes you learn about could impact your business.

Four trends are clear today. The first is that technological advances are miniaturizing many products. Motorola's pocket telephone is an example.

Another is that technological advances usually lead to a decrease in the price of goods. As an example, in the March 1990 issue of *Fortune* magazine, Ralph Gomory, the former head of research at IBM and current president of the Alfred Sloan Foundation, predicted that computers will be 100 times cheaper in the next 20 years.

A third trend is that businesses are applying technology broadly. As an indicator of this you can go into almost any office building and see computers in use.

Finally, technology is becoming increasingly user-friendly. In no time, we should be able to telephone our VCRs to tell them we'll be a little late so that they should tape our favorite television shows.

There are several ways to track technological advances. If you are lucky enough to be a true "techie" (i.e., you **love** to read about technology, talk about it, tinker with it), then you can just keep reading what you are reading, talking about what you are talking about, and tinkering with what you are tinkering. If you aren't a techie, it is time to start skimming technology-related magazines and make it a point to regularly roam computer, telephone, and communication stores where you can see the changes. If the stores are quiet, you might want to strike up a conversation with one of the salespeople; the good ones are always techies and have a good grasp of what is going on.

Exercise 3-3

List below the technology trends you have discovered that could impact your business.

TECHNOLOGY TRENDS

TREND	IMPACT

Now is a good time to summarize what you have discovered in this chapter. Your summary is the situational analysis section of a market plan. You can write it in the space provided. Be sure to include some comments about how each environment will impact the sales of your product (hopefully in a positive way). An example of a situational analysis is included below as a model.

Example: Situational Analysis

ABC Recycling Plant

Introduction: Overall, the situation for ABC's new product is good. The national economy is experiencing slow growth. As the national debt decreases and financial institutions relax, more contracts will become available.

The recycling industry is growing at better than 20 percent per year, mostly as a result of the increase in demand for recycling plants.

Politically and culturally there is an increasing concern with waste in general and plastic wastes in particular.

Legally, more and more local state governments are mandating recycling for both households and businesses.

Finally, consumers seem increasingly to be willing to recycle. In sixteen major U.S. cities, recycling has increased by 40 percent in the past three years as the "greening of America" movement has taken hold.

Economic Trends

All national economic trends are positive. Inflation is expected to be less than 5 percent through 1995, while the GDP is expected to increase by that amount on an annual basis. Contracts and orders for new plant equipment have increased moderately in the past three years; this is expected to continue. The unemployment rate is low, at 4 percent. Finally, for the foreseeable future, interest rates are expected to stabilize at no more than one or two points above the prime lending rate.

As for the recycling industry, the demand for recycling plants has been growing at better than 20 percent per year. Government regulations continue to slow the introduction of new technology in the industry, resulting in market introduction of new technology five to seven years after the development of the technology. Market trends suggest that customers will shift from Fortune 500 companies to partnerships between smaller companies with incomes that are more than $50 million per year. State and regional governments also are expected to be an increasing customer base. The geographical concentration is expected to be in the northeast, Midwest and far west, where there are concentrations of industry and population.

The Legal Environment

All recycling plants are regulated closely and monitored by the Environmental Protection Agency and the Department of Natural Resources in each state. This is expected to both continue and increase in the California region, where regional coalitions of governments regulate recycling plants. The same is true for virtually all of New England. There is increasing evidence that cities are also enacting regulations related to recycling plants, implying that no specific plans should be made for construction without a site visit to local government agencies regarding appropriate permits.

There is some indication that liability insurance rates could increase significantly in the next three years. Since 1985, rates have increased by 100 percent. Our public affairs staff have been told by insurance industry representatives that an additional 100 percent increase could take place before 1995. We have estimated this probability at better than 60 percent.

Social and Cultural Trends

The U.S. population has become very sensitive to environmental issues. In May 1990, national polls found that 75 percent of respondents classified themselves as environmentalists. This concern is strongest among "baby boomers" and the more than 30 million Americans older than 65. Public and private elementary schools are integrating environmental education into their curriculum. This concern is expected to increase. As a result, there has been an upsurge in bond issues for recycling plants in local areas, with most activity taking place in cities where there are universities. A possible softness in the market could result from increased consumer awareness as well. There is a strong movement toward glass and plastic reuse, notably in the food industry. This could result in a decrease in the tonnage needing to be recycled by plants.

Technological Trends

Technological advances are making two things possible. A wide variety of substances can now be separated at one site at the same time. Smaller plants (one-fourth the size of original recycling plants built in the 1960s) also are feasible. Costs for construction are decreasing. Finally, many of the advances in factory automation, such as computer aided manufacturing, are applicable to recycling.

To summarize, a situational analysis suggests that 1991 is an excellent year to expand ABC through the construction of the ABC Plastic Recycling Plant. The company needs to pay attention to obtaining all necessary building and other permits prior to obtaining expansion financing.

Exercise 3-4

Summarize your situational analysis here.

INTRODUCTION

_____

_____

_____

_____

_____

ECONOMIC TRENDS

_____

_____

_____

_____

_____

_____

LEGAL ENVIRONMENT

_____

_____

_____

_____

_____

_____

SOCIO-CULTURAL ENVIRONMENT

_____

_____

_____

_____

_____

_____

TECHNOLOGICAL TRENDS

_____

_____

_____

_____

_____

_____

SUMMARY

_____

_____

_____

_____

_____

_____

What Is a Market?
Or,
Will Anyone Buy
This Product?

Step Four: Wrapping Your Arms Around a Market

One of the unfortunate truths about marketing is the importance of really understanding key marketing concepts before you actually sit down to start the process of deciding to whom you want to sell your product. One of the most difficult concepts, which is also the most financially rewarding once you understand it, is niche marketing. Already on *Business Week's* list of what's "in" for the '90s, niche marketing is the opposite of trying to be all things to all people. Instead, it is an act of courage on the part of most entrepreneurs because it really constitutes a decision to aim your products at a small—but well defined—part of a bigger market that everyone else seems to have overlooked.

Here are some examples of niche markets:

✦ Diet cat food for fat cats, which represents about 20 percent of a $5.9 billion U.S. market;

✦ Fiberglass cabinets for medical equipment;

✦ Micro-magic frozen foods; and

✦ Organic tomato sauce.

I became a real believer in niche marketing several years ago when a woman in one of my seminars announced to the group that she was opening a clothing store for women in a small town in Michigan. Trying not to discourage her, I calmly recited all the reasons why that might not be the best investment of her time, not to mention money. The list included low, often non-existent margins on sales, which meant that she would be lucky to break even; intense competition from surrounding shopping malls; and her location, which, I patiently explained, was exactly wrong because there would be little traffic coming her way. To her credit, the woman heard me out before she described the store. Her market research had shown a sizeable market for professional clothes for women under five feet tall who wear size 12-18 clothing. In fact, such clothes are virtually non-existent in most retail stores.

Now, that is an example of a perfect niche market. It is a small, definable part of a larger market, i.e., professional clothes for women, which has been overlooked by the competition. Since then, my own market research on her idea has substantiated everything she told me at the seminar. There is a market; it is significant; and women are willing to drive up to 60 miles to find fashionable clothes that really fit. The moral of this story is that it will be important to narrow your focus regarding potential customers even as you start to define them.

This can be a painful task because in some ways, it is counter intuitive. Most business owners and sales people tend to believe that the key is broad exposure to everyone. In other words, if you somehow let the world know about your product, the sales will follow. The right people will find their way to your product. Wrong. Customers increasingly are particular about their needs, and this trend won't slow down in any of our lifetimes. Generic products just won't do. Focus will become increasing critical through the 1990s as all our markets become global.

Advantages of Niche Marketing

There are significant advantages to a focused marketing approach as opposed to trying to market your product to every possible customer:

1. If you are successful, it gives you strong customer loyalty. As I get older and more health conscious, I find myself reading food labels in a way that I never would have predicted. This exercise has identified several food companies who consistently have top quality ingredients. As one example, Eden Foods tries to use organic ingredients whenever possible and has, over time, increased the amount of organic ingredients in its products. As a result, I tend to look for their products whenever I shop. In other words, I have become a loyal member of their niche market— consumers increasingly concerned about the quality of the ingredients of their food.

2. Niche marketing gives you a head start into a market. In marketing terminology, this is called a "beach head." In 1990, Heinz Pet Products announced Lean Entrees, a 95 percent fat-free canned cat food. It is the first national line of diet cat food, giving the company a real head start into what could be a $1.2 billion market.

3. Niche marketing gives you a market position from which you can make further penetrations into the market you've defined. Eden

Foods can expand into other types of healthy food, and Heinz can move into the diet dog food market or the diet pet pig food market.

4. Because you are more likely to have customer loyalty than companies trying to be all things to all people, you are more able to hold off the competition. Because I am comfortable with the quality of Eden Foods products, I don't even bother to look at other similar products. Remember, we are creatures of habit more than we are willing to admit. Haven't you noticed that once you find a product that serves you well, you stay with it no matter what its competition does? My father will probably always buy Chryslers. I will always by Pears Soap. My children are still watching the same television shows even though they can mouth the words of some of the re-runs.

5. Niche marketing is usually less expensive to you than a broader market approach because you may need fewer brochures, fewer advertisements, or fewer sales people.

The key to marketing is to very carefully define who your customers will be before you actually put together a market plan. In that process, you will want to develop a way to make certain that these same customers will really want your product once you are out on the street selling it. Most companies use customer surveys, focus groups and other market research to do this. All of these processes will be described in later chapters.

Disadvantages of Niche Marketing

There are two potholes to watch for when you narrow your focus. The first has to do with other markets. In narrowing your focus, you end up ignoring some potential customers. The end result can be missed opportunities for making money. Another pothole has to do with increased marketing costs. If you decide to focus on one niche at a time, you will find that you need a different market plan or strategy for each niche. For example, Coca-Cola needs one market plan for aging baby-boomers who increasingly choose Diet Coke as their breakfast of choice. The company needs an entirely different market plan for adolescent girls who use Diet

Coke as an appetite suppressant. These are two different niches and call for two entirely different advertising, packaging, and sales campaigns.

Let's stay with the Coca-Cola example. The circle above represents many of the people who will drink Coca-Cola. First, think about all their different products and write them into the circle. I've listed the ones I could name.

Now, think abut who buys each type of product. Take Coca-Cola Classic as an example. Several examples of niches are: teenage boys, men who don't drink beer, women who aren't overly concerned about their weight, anyone who doesn't trust sweeteners (health conscious consumers). I'm sure there are many more niches. The point is that each of these groups is different in their buying behavior and in how they get product information. Teenage boys may buy Coke when they are with friends and get their information from radio and MTV. Women may buy Coke as a "treat" at the grocery store because it reminds them of their own teenage years.

Your task will be to think about the potential customers, dividing them into groups or segments that you can then zoom in on—first to study and later to target. In other words, narrowing your focus means taking your total market—all the people or companies that will buy your product—and breaking it into groups of potential buyers so that each group reflects customers having similar needs that are different from other groups of customers.

When is a Niche a Niche?

Now, how will you know when you've really identified a market niche? Here are four criteria for deciding:

1. A group whose reactions to certain marketing tasks are similar but different from other groups represents a niche. For example, most women who are in the first throes of starting a business react very differently to telemarketing than women who have been in business for several years.

2. A group about which there is information is a niche. Data on buying behavior is particularly important. This can be tough when you are trying to market a product to either very low or very high income individuals or to privately held small firms. In other words, your potential customers need to be "researchable."

3. A niche group can be reached through clearly identified channels of distribution. For example, you can get the attention of most children in America today by advertising on Saturday morning television. Thousands of entrepreneurs nationally can be reached through advertisements in *Inc. Magazine*. When I want to get the attention of managers of mid-sized privately held companies in Michigan, I advertise in the weekly business magazine, *Crain's Detroit Business*. I use MTV for pre-teens and teenagers, Arsenio Hall for the "young at heart," and health-related magazines for health food.

4. Finally, the group needs to be big enough to provide enough of a profit to make it worthwhile to target them in the first place. In other words, the number of potential buyers in the segment and their volume of expected purchases is the final measure of whether you have identified a segment worth targeting.

Segment Characteristics

How do you differentiate one person from another or one company from other companies? The good news is that marketing and advertising firms have spent years and billions of dollars coming up with methods of "segmenting" customers. Some major forms of differentiation are listed in the following chart.

EXAMPLES OF SEGMENT CHARACTERISTICS

	Examples of Choices
How the product will be used	• Business
	• Home Business
	• Recreation
	• Education
Type of product	• Convenience Good
	• Specialty Good
	• Functional Product
	• Recreational Product
Demographics of the customer (individual)	• Age
	• Sex
	• Ethnicity
	• Income Level
	• Education Level
	• Social Class
Demographics of the customer (business)	• Sales Level
	• Public/Private
	• Number of Employees
	• Primary Activity
Lifestyle (attitudes, interests, opinions)	• Curious
	• Adventurous
	• Informal
	• Formal
	• Spiritual
	• Structured

Now, you try it. Think about all the possible customers you have for your product and choose a group that you think is most likely to respond to your marketing efforts. Describe the group here, as specifically as you can:

_____

_____

CHAPTER FOUR

Defining Your Market: Using Specific Measurements

Step Five: Getting Started

Given everything covered so far, there is really only one way to begin the process of defining your market, and that is simply to guess. If your business is new or you are starting a new product line, then a good guess is a useful starting point. What are you guessing? Who your customers will be. The format of your guess can be called a "customer profile," made up of attributes that describe your customers as intimately as is legal. You started the guessing process at the end of Chapter Four. This chapter will help you to refine that guess work.

The process of defining your customers is very similar to a search for the perfect mate in that you want to describe all of the characteristics that will later help you to separate potential customers from people or companies who won't ever be customers. The characteristics described in Chapter Four are a useful starting point.

If you already have revenues, this exercise is a little easier because you don't need to guess who your customers will be. Instead, you need to obtain a list of your existing customers, and then analyze the list, looking for shared characteristics. This will help you identify new customers who have the same characteristics. Most people actually have a fairly good sense of who will be most interested in a product once it hits the market. The harder part is to describe the specific characteristics that will help identify the source of your future revenues. The characteristics listed in Exercise 5-1 and 5-2 will help you get started. Use Exercise 5-1 if your potential customers are people and Exercise 5-2 if your potential customers are companies. If you plan to sell to both, fill out both exhibits.

Exercise 5-1: Possible Customer Profile (People)

Income characteristics that matter: (for example, does your customer need to have an income of a specific amount to be able to buy your product?)

_____

_____

_____

_____

_____

Personality traits that matter: (for example, will you sell to people who want the "best" product on the market or to people who have a certain number of years of education before they need your product?)

_____

_____

_____

_____

Buying behavior that matters: (for example, will most of your customers need to purchase your product using a credit card?)

_____

_____

_____

Where do your customers live? (City, county, region, state, etc.)

_____

_____

_____

Are there other characteristics that will help you separate potential customers from non-customers? List them here.

_____

_____

_____

_____

_____

_____

Exercise 5-2: Possible Customer Profile (Companies)

Size characteristics that matter: (for example, do you only want to sell to Fortune 500 Companies or the biggest companies in your industry?)

_____

_____

_____

_____

_____

Revenue characteristics that matter: (for example, do you think your customers will fall within a certain revenue range, say $2 million to $10 million a year?)

_____

_____

_____

_____

What business will your customers represent?

_____

_____

_____

_____

Where will they be based? (City, county, state, region, etc.)

_____

_____

_____

_____

Are there other characteristics that will help you to separate potential customers from non-customers? List them here.

_____

_____

_____

_____

_____

_____

_____

K ey Market Attributes: What Are They?

One of the saddest truths about business is that nobody can sell their product to everyone all the time. Actually, the news is even worse: Nobody, with the possible exception of Coca-Cola and Sony, can sell their product to their entire market at the same time. It is simply too expensive and complicated. In marketing, that means that your first step is to describe, in great detail, the chunk of the population that you think is most likely to buy your product.

Like people, all markets have attributes. Before you can describe individual customers correctly, you must place them within a context. That context is your niche, which we discussed in Chapter Four. The exercise is like describing a community; once you describe the community, you can make an accurate estimate regarding the members of that community. Instead of descriptions such as "short," "tall," "heavy," "thin," "pretty," "smart," markets can be described in other terms:

◆ Size, either in terms of money or units;

◆ Rate of growth;

◆ Age; how old the market is;

✦ Diversity; i.e., whether the market includes lots of parts which are different or many parts that are similar;

✦ Sensitivity to outside factors such as government regulations;

✦ Sensitivity to price;

✦ Seasonality;

✦ Cliques;

✦ Penetrability; i.e. ease of entering the market with a new product; and

✦ The amount of technology involved in the market.

Once you have made your first guesses about the characteristics of your potential customers, you can start to zero in on the attributes of your market as a whole. The key here is to try to identify as many attributes as you can. Remember that the more precisely you define your market, the more you will be able to rule out all those people and companies who are not potential clients. As a result, you will save time and energy that would be wasted on the wrong people or companies. Even better, you will also save money.

To begin defining your market's attributes, first gather information about the market from a multitude of sources. As mentioned earlier, all sorts of statistics are available from the U.S. Department of Commerce, notably in its *Annual Outlook on U.S. Industries*. The major journals for your industry also will have a great deal of information, as will trade associations. Most industry journals have an annual issue in which they describe industry trends in great detail. *Forbes* or *Fortune* do annual overviews of the major industries. The *New York Times*, *Barrons*, and *The Wall Street Journal* are also useful sources of industry data, assuming you can skim them by using some type of computerized index located at a public or university library. These all can be useful starting points. Take time to read as much as you can about what is going on in your industry.

While you do so, it is useful to keep a list of all the sources of information that helped you describe your market, and then keep that list in a safe place. You never know when you'll need to retrace your thinking. Exercise 5-3 will help with this.

Exercise 5-3

SOURCES OF MARKET INFORMATION

TITLE OF SOURCE	WHERE FOUND	USED FOR
Example: U.S. Dept. of Commerce Annual Industry Outlook	public library, university, business school	identify market attributes

Once you have reviewed resources that describe your industry, you should be ready to describe your market. Each attribute is discussed below along with an example of how a description could be worded.

Size

This usually comes from market forecasts in industry journals. If market forecasts are unclear to you, here is a definition: market forecasts are estimates of the dollar or unit sales of a product or product line for all firms within a certain period of time. In other words, it is the actual expected sales for a product for all firms selling the same product in a certain industry.

You can start thinking about the actual sales potential for your product here, as well. The sales potential is the amount of sales you think you can really make in a given period of time. (Optimists take note—whatever you have estimated, cut it by at least a third. Trust me on this one).

What is the size of the market in dollars?

Example: $15 billion was spent on motivational marketing programs last year, an increase of 15 percent over 1990.

What is the size of the market in units?

Example: 1,500 motivational workshops are held in the United States every year.

Rate of Growth

The growth rate of a market is critical because you want to be in a market that is growing. The reason for this is that growth usually allows everybody in the market to increase their sales without attacking each other too directly. If the market is not growing, competition will respond to your market entrance by lowering their prices and going after your reputation—or worse.

What is the market's rate of growth?

Example: The growth rate for this market has been 15 percent per year since 1980, up from 10 percent per year in the period 1970 to 1979.

Age

Age is important because every product has a life cycle. In its "childhood" years, a product tends to be used by innovators, i.e., people or companies who like to experiment. Usually, there are not too many of those who can make the financial viability of your product questionable. In its "adolescence" and "early adulthood," more and more customers will want the product. Unfortunately, once the product has reached a maturity stage, sales can drop off significantly. Sometimes the drop is because new competitive products have been introduced to the market. More often, most potential customers either have the product, buy it regularly, or they've become tired of it. Your goal should be to develop products aimed at a fairly young market so that you can earn revenue for longer.

How old is the market?

Example: The personal computer market is eleven years old, meaning that several generations of products have now been developed and market-tested.

Diversity

Diversity, or market breadth, is also critical. Some products can be used for a variety of functions. These are products aimed at diverse markets. Other products are developed specifically for one function in one market. This is a narrow market product.

How diverse is the market?

Example: Although large, the medical market for aminoassays is narrowly defined.

OR: The market for monogrammed leather is diverse, ranging from leather upholstery to children's sandals.

Sensitivity to Outside Factors

Although all products are somewhat sensitive to outside factors, they vary in sensitivity. In a perfect world, you would find a chunk of the population that would buy your product no matter what was happening politically, economically, or environmentally. Unfortunately, no such market exists. Given reality, you want to try to identify a market that is the least sensitive to outside factors and then describe these sensitivities. The question to ask yourself is, "How sensitive is the market to legal, political, social, cultural, technological, and environmental factors?"

How sensitive is the market to outside factors?

Example: The growth of the pizza market in China continues to depend on trade regulations under development by the Chinese national government.

Sensitivity to Price Changes

Different markets also differ in how sensitive they are to changes in product price. For example, historically Mercedes buyers haven't seemed to be too concerned with price increases. When you want a Mercedes, you want a Mercedes. On the other hand, many retail products manufacturers find that small increases in price result in fewer purchases, often combined with a loss of customers to their competition. To determine whether your market is price sensitive, check out its buying behavior over the past three to five years. Have more products been purchased as prices decreased? Did fewer purchases result from price increases? If you can't find statistics, ask salespeople in the industry, they'll know whether your market is price sensitive.

How sensitive is the market to price changes?

Example: In the past five years, the market has been declining in terms of product sold by a minimum of 10 percent for every increase in price of 20 percent or more. Or this market is so young that variations in prices of up to 100 percent are not impacting buyer trends.

Seasonality

One of the biggest surprises about market behavior is that most markets are seasonal. People or companies will tend to purchase products at certain times of the year. In fact, my experience has been that virtually all markets are seasonal. Assume seasonality until you learn otherwise.
How seasonal is the market?

Example: The market for swimming pool disinfectants is seasonal in 70 percent of the United States. In this geographical area, 80 percent of purchases are made in the five months of May, June, July, August, and September.

Cliques

Cliques can be important to your market strategy. If a few companies are calling all the shots, i.e., setting standards or price and delivery strategies, then your market is controlled by cliques. You need to be able to play by their rules if you are going to sell your product.

Is your market controlled by a small group of companies? If so, which?

Example: Until recently, the automobile market in the United States was controlled by General Motors, Ford, and Chrysler. This has changed drastically over the past ten years as European, Japanese, and Korean automotive products have become increasingly competitive.

Penetrability

Ease of penetration has to do with how difficult it is to introduce a product to the market. A good rule of thumb is that the more regulated the industry, the tougher it is to enter the market. Barriers to entry can be anything from patents to high training costs to technological advances peculiar to the product. Your goal should be to try to be able to pay the price to get past a barrier so that your company can have an edge over competing products.

How easy is it to enter your market?

Example: Because this product is regulated by the Food and Drug Administration, and because it now takes up to four years for FDA approval, entry into the market could be difficult.

Technology Involved

The level of technology involved in your product's production and use may be important to your market. This has significant implications because the more technology involved, the harder it is to get into the market. Technology also means you'll need to support your product with additional services, (such as teaching people how to use it and being ready to service it around the clock).

How much technology is involved in your market?

Example: The computer disk market is entirely technology driven.

The following is a sample discussion of attributes for the management training seminars market. It is followed by Exercise 5-4, a worksheet you can use to define your own market's attributes.

Example: Market Attributes

DEF Management Training Seminars, Inc.

The present market size for Management Training Seminars Inc. is $20 billion per year in the United States and Canada. This includes training for professionals in management, strategic planning, marketing, and financial analysis. The market for our seminars is diverse, ranging from individual professionals, and entrepreneurs to senior management teams from Fortune 500 Corporations. Industry experts predict that the market will increase at a slow but steady 3 percent to 5 percent growth per year. The seminar market is a mature market. Although there was significant growth in the 1980s, this has slowed significantly suggesting that new products may be needed to hold onto DEF's share of the market.

Seminars have become increasingly sensitive to outside factors. Economic down trends tend to cause a drop of 10 percent to 20 percent in seminar attendance, depending on the size of the down trend. On the other hand, increased regulations related to personnel issues and product liability have resulted in increased seminar attendance for sessions on managing people and customer relations.

This market is also sensitive to pricing for seminars priced at $200 or more. Below that amount there is no discernible price sensitivity. Above that amount, seminar registrations decrease by up to 50 percent for every incremental increase in price of $100 for all types of seminars.

The seminar market is extremely seasonal. Attendance is highest between September 15 and November 15, and between January 15 and April 15th. Participation drops off dramatically in the summer months and over the Christmas season.

The seminar market is not controlled by cliques. Instead, most educational institutions of higher learning, such as community colleges, offer a variety of management seminars, as do accounting and management consulting firms. Professional associations such as the American Marketing Association offer a wide variety of seminars for professionals. Recently, companies such as Careertrak in Boulder, Colorado, have emerged as market leaders in low cost ($99 per seminar), one-day management seminars. As a result of all these players, penetrating the market, i.e., offering a seminar, is relatively easy. On the other hand, the number of seminars offered makes it difficult for a new company without name recognition to penetrate the market successfully. In other words, seminars may be offered, but no one will come.

Exercise 5-4: Market Attributes

What is the size of your market in dollars or units or both?

_____

_____

_____

What is the growth rate of your market?

_____

_____

_____

How old is the market?

_____

_____

_____

How diverse is the market?

_____

_____

_____

_____

How sensitive is the market to outside factors?

_____

_____

_____

How sensitive is the market to price changes?

_____

_____

_____

How seasonal is the market? What are the patterns?

_____

_____

_____

Is the market controlled by a clique?

_____

_____

_____

How difficult is it to penetrate your market?

_____

_____

_____

What technologies are involved in your market?

_____

_____

_____

Customer Profiles— People

Once you have defined the attributes of your market as a whole, you can begin to zero in on your customers as individuals. If you are selling your product to people, you can describe them using the following characteristics: age, sex, race, income, education level, political inclination, employment, geographical area, buying behavior.

Age

This is usually done in age groups. Example:

Elderly = 65+
Advanced middle age = 61-65
Middle age = 51-60
Beginning middle age = 35-50
Teen/post-teen = 13-21
Adolescent = 7-12
Child = 2-6
Baby = 0-2

Sex

So far there are only two; male and female - but who knows what the future might bring.

Race

Ranges could include:

African-American
Asian
Caucasian
Hispanic
Native American
Other

Income

Ranges could include:

Under $5,000
$5,000-9,999
$10,000-14,999
$15,000-29,999
$30,000-49,999
$50,000-69,999
$70,000-99,999
$100,000+

Education Level

Ranges could include:

Below high school
Some high school
High school graduate
Some college
Associate's degree
Bachelor's degree
Some graduate school
Advanced degree

Political Inclination

This can be Republican, Democrat, Independent, or a host of other political affiliations.

Employment

Ranges could include:

Homemaker
Student
Self-employed
Service
Retail
Manufacturing

This category can also be split up into professional versus non-professional.

Geographical Area

You can define this as a city, county, state, region, or nation, depending on what is most useful for your purposes.

Buying Behavior

You will want to use patterns for your industry. For example, most people finance the purchase of their automobiles. Most teenagers buy clothes with cash; their parents use credit cards.

Other Attributes

The following example may suggest other areas pertinent to your market attribute evaluation.

POSSIBLE MARKET ATTRIBUTES

Activities Related to:	Interests Related to:	Opinions Related to:
Demographics	Work	Family
Themselves	Age	Hobbies
Home	Social Issues	Education
Vacation	Community	Business
Occupation	Entertainment	Recreation
Economics	Family Size	Clubs
Fashion	Education	Dwelling
Community	Food	Products
Geography	Shopping	Media
Future	City Size	Sports
Achievements	Culture	Life Stage

Adapted from Joe T. Plummer, "The Concept and Application of Life Style Segmentation," *Journal of Marketing* Vol. 38, No. 1 (Jan. 1974), p. 34. Reprinted with permission of the American Marketing Association.

Now you try it. Use Exercise 5-5 to fill in your customers attributes if your customers are individuals.

Exercise 5-5: Customer Profile (People)

AGE _____

_____

SEX _____

_____

RACE _____

_____

INCOME _____

_____

EDUCATION _____

_____

POLITICS _____

_____

EMPLOYMENT _____

_____

GEOGRAPHIC AREA _____

_____

BUYING BEHAVIOR _____

_____

OTHER _____

_____

_____

_____

_____

_____

Customer Profiles— Companies

As customers, companies have their own set of characteristics. Some of these include:

Age of the company
Size in employees
Revenues
Profitability
Product lines
R&D expenditures
Their geographical market
Purchasing process
Buying behavior

Age of the Company

This can be broken down into mature companies, of ten operational years or more; young companies, from three to ten operational years; or emerging companies, from start-up to three years of operation.

Size in Employees

This could be classified as:

Over 1,000
500-1,000
100-500
50-100
20-50
3-20
1-3
Self-employed

Revenues

This could be classified as:

Start-up
Under $50,000
Under $100,000
Under $500,000

Under $1 million
Under $10 million
Under $50 million
Under $100 million, etc.

Profitability

This can range from no profit to high profits. You will want to define what you consider high or low profits. What you are after is the company's track record for profitability:

High profits
Profits reflecting the industry's average
Low profits
Profits less than the industry's average
No profits

Product Lines

This is made up of the products your customers sell, and can be described by Standard Industry Classification (SIC) codes. This is a standardized industrial coding system used to categorize virtually all industries. A summary of SIC categories can be found in the following list. For a more complete listing, head for your local public library.

Example: General SIC Categories

0000-0999	Agriculture, Forestry, Fishing
1000-1499	Mining
1500-1799	Construction
2000-3999	Manufacturing
4000-4999	Transportation and Public Utilities
5000-5199	Wholesale Trade
5200-5999	Retail Trade
6000-6799	Finance, Insurance and Real Estate
7000-8999	Services
9000-9600	Public Sector

R&D Expenditures

This usually matters in cases where you are selling a technology-based product or a product that is the first of its kind. The more companies spend on R&D, relative to other expenses (and relative to other companies in your industry), the more likely they are to try new things. Possible categories are:

> More than 5 percent of operating expenses
>
> One percent to 5 percent of operating expenses
>
> No R&D expenses
>
> Geographical market

This section simply describes where your customers currently sell their own products.

Purchasing Process

This tends to be idiosyncratic to particular industries. If different companies in your market have different types of purchasing processes, you need to define them in order to decide which group you will approach first. Included would be whether you need to respond to a bidding process or at what management level within the company you need to sell your product.

Buying Behavior

This can be any pertinent characteristic that would help you to identify companies you want to approach now from companies you can target later. Examples include the length of time it take to get a positive decision from the company to buy your product, whether under-the-counter payments are expected, whether the president needs to approve every purchase, etc.

Use Exercise 5-6 to fill in your customers attributes if your customers are companies.

Exercise 5-6: Customer Profile (Companies)

AGE _____

_____

SIZE IN EMPLOYEES _____

_____

PROFITABILITY _____

_____

TYPE OF BUSINESS _____

_____

PRODUCT LINES _____

_____

R&D EXPENDITURES _____

_____

GEOGRAPHICAL MARKET _____

_____

PURCHASING PROCESS _____

_____

BUYING BEHAVIOR _____

_____

_____

_____

_____

_____

_____

_____

Choosing the Characteristics that Define Your Customers

The last step in defining your market is to choose which characteristics will be used as the basis for your target market. To do this, review your company profiles, and select the attributes that are most pertinent to your product. For example, if it does not matter to you whether your customer is male or female, you can rule out sex as a screening test for whether or not you should spend time selling to someone. You will want to choose characteristics that will help to identify quickly and easily who you do NOT want as customers. They also should be characteristics that will help you to get to the people/companies most likely to give your product fast approval. In other words, focus on characteristics that will provide the fastest sales.

As you start selling your product, you will find that you may need to add or drop some characteristics, or change your customer descriptions in other ways. That is the nature of marketing. What is important to remember is to keep your profile updated through time so that it can always be used as a screen for those people or companies to which you do not need to spend time selling.

Chapter Six

Tuning Your
Market Definition

Zeroing in on Your Target Market

By now, you should have come to the conclusion that most of marketing has to do with research, research, and more research. It's true. The more research you can do to identify your customers and their buying behavior—before you start to sell—the better off you will be. Just when you think you've identified your target market, you need to break it down even more.

Remember, in Chapter Five you developed a profile of the market. As your sixth step, you will see that you can further segment your market. Here's an example from my own work. Three years ago, I decided that I wanted to focus on women business owners for one of our business planning products. The original customer profile looked something like this:

Example: Customer Profile

Product: Business plans

Customer Profile: Women-owned businesses

Age: Companies less than 20 years old

Revenues: Up to $20 million in sales

Size: Less than 500 employees

Profitability: Profitable, or have alternative sources of revenue to pay for assistance

Type of Business: Service or manufacturing

Product Lines: SIC codes 2000-3999 Manufacturing and 7000-8999 Services

R&D Expenditures: Not applicable

Purchasing Process: CEO makes the decision to buy

Buying Behavior: Decision can be made within a three-month period; CEO is accessible

Geography: Headquartered in the Midwest states

Although I have now defined a niche market, I can break it down even further into a number of smaller target groupings.

Example: Market Segments

As you study the example on the following pages, you'll see that the segments I've identified are significantly different, even though each one fits within the original target market. This is analogous to a family; even though the children may come from the same parents, they will have identifiable differences that allow outsiders to separate them from each other.

A written description of each of the segments might go like this:

Segment I is made up of relatively young, successful female-owned service companies in Michigan. These are often spin-off companies from larger service companies or franchises.

Segment II is made up of older manufacturing companies in Michigan. These often are owned jointly by spouses or siblings, or are companies women have inherited from their parents.

Segment III is made up of young, fast-growing female-owned and smart service companies in Michigan. These are often technology-based, even though they are service firms. Examples would include computer services and medical-related temporary firms.

Segment IV is made up of young, fast-growing, female-owned and smart manufacturing companies in Michigan. These often are related to the automobile industry and reflect recently awarded supplier contracts in the industry.

Segment V is made up of start-up, female-owned service companies in Michigan. This is a broad category and represents everything from pet-sitting to service franchises to marketing consultants.

Segment VI is made up of start-up, female-owned manufacturing companies in Michigan. This is also a fairly broad category and represents everything from a family-owned tool & die shop to a company that manufactures hand-painted t-shirts for craft fairs.

Segments VII through XII represent the same categories in Ohio and XIII through XVIII represent those categories in Indiana.

MARKET SEGMENTS

CHARACTERISTIC	TARGET MARKET	I	II	III	IV	V	VI
AGE	Under 20 years	3–10	10–20	0–3	0–3	0–3	0–3
REVENUES	Up to $20 million	$3 mil +	$10–20	up to $10	up to $10	up to $1	up to $1
PROFITABILITY	Profitable						
EMPLOYEES	Up to 500	n/a	more than 50	less than 50	less than 50	less than 50	less than 50
TYPE OF BUSINESS	SVC or MFG	SVC	MFG	SVC	MFG	SVC	MFG
PRODUCT LINES	2000–3999 7000–8999	7000–8999	2000–3999	7000–8999	2000–3999	7000–8999	2000–3999
R&D EXPENDITURES	Not applicable	n/a	some	n/a	n/a	some	some
PURCHASING PROCESS	CEO decides	CEO	CEO	CEO	CEO	CEO	CEO
BUYING BEHAVIOR	Within 3 months	3 mo	3 mo	3 mo	3 mo	3 mo	3 mo
GEOGRAPHY	Michigan, Ohio, or Indiana	MI	MI	MI	MI	MI	MI

MARKET SEGMENTS

CHARACTERISTIC	TARGET MARKET	VII	VIII	IX	X	XI	XII
AGE	Under 20 years	3–10	10–20	0–3	0–3	0–3	0–3
REVENUES	Up to $20 million	$3 mil +	$10–20	up to $10	up to $10	up to $1	up to $1
PROFITABILITY	Profitable						
EMPLOYEES	Up to 500	n/a	more than 50	less than 50	less than 50	less than 50	less than 50
TYPE OF BUSINESS	SVC or MFG	SVC	MFG	SVC	MFG	SVC	MFG
PRODUCT LINES	2000–3999 7000–8999	7000–8999	2000–3999	7000–8999	2000–3999	7000–8999	2000–3999
R&D EXPENDITURES	Not applicable	n/a	some	n/a	n/a	some	some
PURCHASING PROCESS	CEO decides	CEO	CEO	CEO	CEO	CEO	CEO
BUYING BEHAVIOR	Within 3 months	3 mo	3 mo	3 mo	3 mo	3 mo	3 mo
GEOGRAPHY	Michigan, Ohio, or Indiana	OH	OH	OH	OH	OH	OH

MARKET SEGMENTS

CHARACTERISTIC	TARGET MARKET	XIII	XIV	XV	XVI	XVII	XVIII
AGE	Under 20 years	3–10	10–20	0–3	0–3	0–3	0–3
REVENUES	Up to $20 million	$3 mil +	$10–20	up to $10	up to $10	up to $1	up to $1
PROFITABILITY	Profitable						
EMPLOYEES	Up to 500	n/a	more than 50	less than 50	less than 50	less than 50	less than 50
TYPE OF BUSINESS	SVC or MFG	SVC	MFG	SVC	MFG	SVC	MFG
PRODUCT LINES	2000–3999 7000–8999	7000–8999	2000–3999	7000–8999	2000–3999	7000–8999	2000–3999
R&D EXPENDITURES	Not applicable	n/a	some	n/a	n/a	some	some
PURCHASING PROCESS	CEO decides	CEO	CEO	CEO	CEO	CEO	CEO
BUYING BEHAVIOR	Within 3 months	3 mo	3 mo	3 mo	3 mo	3 mo	3 mo
GEOGRAPHY	Michigan, Ohio, or Indiana	IN	IN	IN	IN	IN	IN

A picture of the fine tuning or segmentation just completed would look like this:

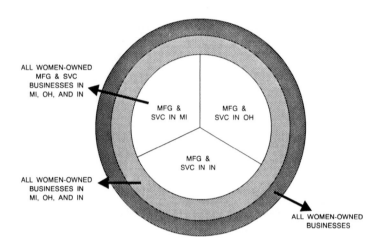

A further blow-up of the Michigan segment would look like the following:

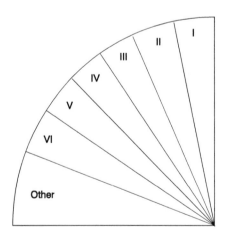

Women-Owned Businesses in Michigan
in the Manufacturing and Service Industries

How to Verify that You've Identified Segments

Once you have fine tuned your market into target segments, the following checklist will help you to decide whether or not you have identified a true target segment. For each segment, you should be able to answer yes to the following ten questions.

Is the segment specific? In other words, when you meet a potential customer, will he or she obviously fit into one of your segments?

Is the segment measurable in units? To put it differently, is there a way to find out how many customers are in the segment?

Is the segment measurable in dollars?

Does the segment have growth potential?

Is the segment economically accessible? In other words, can you afford to get the attention of the people or companies to whom you want to sell at a cost you can afford?

Is the segment stable? In other words, if it takes six months to a year to get your marketing strategy together, will they still be there?

Whenever your answer wasn't a resounding "yes," you will need to rethink how you want to define the segment until you can say yes.

Other Behavior Characteristics

Here are some ways to use segment characteristics to divide the world into potential customers and non-customers. Looking at product use, people who buy personal computers tend to buy them for different reasons. Some people purchase them for home office use. Market analysts tell us that this group is increasing in number. Other people purchase them for pleasure, i.e. to write letters, poems, the book they've had in their head for twenty years, etc. Yet another group may purchase them for their children. Each of these buyer types represents a different niche, because their reasons for purchasing a computer are different. As a result, they will respond to you in different ways. For example, the first group might not care if the computer keys are easily washable. On the other hand, the third group will care because cleaning the keyboard will be an ongoing chore.

As another example of the importance of characteristics, I have noticed that larger companies (more than 50 employees) purchase products differently than smaller companies. For smaller companies, the president is the decision maker for virtually all purchases. As companies increase in size, however, the number of levels of decision makers increases, i.e. more employees need to say yes to your product for you to make the sale. This is an example of a demographic characteristic.

Looking at lifestyle differences, more and more futurists are starting to identify a niche of people who value leisure activities over almost everything else in their lives. Among that group is a subset of folks who have been labeled as "high income, curious." Several major hotel chains have recognized that this niche could be a real money maker and have developed specific products aimed at what I call "adventuresome high-enders." I have been told of one hotel that offers its guests a Ferrari to drive around a test track built right into the hotel complex; water lovers can rent trained dolphins to "buddy-swim" around a man-made coral reef.

As an example of other behavioral characteristics that could be important to a niche, I've noticed that I purchase Diet Pepsi because I believe that it helps me to stay thinner than I would be if I did not drink it. I also believe that, in addition to keeping my breath fresh, my particular brand of toothpaste keeps my teeth whiter.

An Example of Successful Target Marketing

Examples of successful niche marketing are everywhere. In every case I know of, the person who identified the market went through all of the exercises we've covered so far.

One of the most telling stories I've read is about a water pump company that was started about ten years ago. In their wisdom, the owners decided not to sell the pumps to everyone who might need a pump and instead analyzed four industries known to use water pumps: chemicals, petrochemicals, steel, and paper. Their analysis showed that the steel and chemical industries were pretty stagnant at less than 3 percent growth per year. On the other hand, the petrochemical and paper industries were both experiencing better than 10 percent growth per year. Because the petrochemical industry was growing at closer to 30 percent per year, the owners decided to stay clear of that industry because the competition would probably be too intense.

When they took a closer look at the paper industry, they discovered solid growth and very few competitors. In fact, only three companies supplied pumps to that industry. So they took an even closer look and found that while the three competitors had tied up the spare parts business, there was very little competition in new pumps. Better yet, they found that plant engineers were being neglected by the three competitors. As a result, the pump company decided that it would sell price competitive new and spare parts, focusing on plant engineers. In their sales strategy, they emphasized price, responsiveness, and quick delivery. As a result, they grew by 50 percent and ended up with a 90 percent share of the spare parts market in the paper industry.

Another Successful Marketing Story

The Rodale Press was started in 1942 by a fellow named J.I. Rodale. Its first product was a magazine called *Organic Farming and Gardening*. In about 1950, the company started publishing a second magazine, *Prevention*, which now has a circulation of about 3 million. The company identified its niche as "health and fitness" and has only added to its market line when the products are aimed at promoting those two attributes. In 1977, the company added *Bicycling* to its line; in 1985 it bought *Runner's World*. *Men's Health* magazine was started in 1986 and *BackPacker* was purchased in 1988. The company also has a book division with somewhere around 300 titles in print, and it operates several book clubs. What is the result of focusing on a specific segment, such as health and fitness lovers?

According to the president of Rodale Press, the company is growing at close to 15 percent a year, which constitutes tremendous (bordering on miraculous) growth for the publishing industry. Given market trends, Rodale's future should only get better.

Verify Your Niche

To summarize, niche or segment marketing is a marketing world view that makes sense for the nineties. Consumers, whether they are people or companies, are segmenting themselves into more and more different types of groups.

To be successful in marketing, you need to learn how to identify those groups. Then you need to analyze whether or not they are under-served enough by your competition to make a run for them. One of the most difficult tasks in marketing can be deciding whether or not you're actually successful at niche marketing. Even though there are many tests to show if you've identified a niche correctly, you probably can relax you can answer "yes" to the following:

Am I becoming increasingly successful in competitive situations where I am selling to people or companies who are members of the segment I have identified?

Am I getting an increasing number of phone calls from prospective clients even though I've never marketed to them directly?

Is an increasingly large number of business associates *correctly* introducing me and my product line to prospective clients?

When I'm in competitive situations, am I seeing that price is not the main consideration of my potential customers when they choose my firm?

Am I getting an increasing number of referrals from existing customers?

Is the media starting to identify me and my business correctly without interviewing me first?

Does marketing to segments work? You bet. It's a rifle shot instead of a scatter shot. It is more important than any other single marketing strategy you choose. If Evian can successfully sell water that is unflavored, un-filtered, and to my knowledge, un-anything-ed at more than $1.50 per bottle by targeting its product to "hard-bodies," you also will benefit from niche marketing.

Example: Target Segment

The target market for *Managing for Growth* seminars in the state of Florida is made up of managers in companies with annual sales between $500,000 and $10 million, and annual growth rates of 6 percent or better. These managers can be approached through American Management Association memberships, and a series of three advertisements in the business section of their Sunday papers.

Nitty Gritty Research

Step Seven: Customer Surveys

We usually think we know more about our customers than we really do. The only way to be certain that you have targeted people or companies appropriately is to ask them. If you can afford to, it is always worthwhile to survey your customers and/or potential customers.

Many companies find out information about their markets by interviewing people that they believe are potential customers to get their reactions to the product in question. The interviewing process, who to interview and what type of interview to use, can be tricky. There are basically three ways to get direct information about your customers:

Mail interview: a questionnaire is mailed to potential customers.

Telephone interview: you or someone you pay (and trust) ask potential customers questions over the phone.

Personal interview: you, or someone on your staff, talk directly to potential customers, asking specific questions that will lead to answers you need about your product.

Each type of interview has both positive and negative aspects, which are listed below. Once you review these, you can choose which will work best for you, given the type of customers you have, your budget and the time you have to get feedback, as well as the number of people you have helping you. Remember that is virtually impossible to gather too much information about potential customers and the information you gather now could save you millions of dollars later. Much of this chapter is based on a terrific, now classic, survey text, *Mail and Telephone Surveys: Total Design Method* by Don Dillman. If you decide to do your own survey you should go find it.

Mail Interview

Positive

Least expense method; respondents can take their time to think; frank responses on sensitive issues are more likely; can get to virtually all households.

Negative

Least reliable method; non-response can be a problem (as low as 10 percent response rate); can't control who responds.

Telephone Interview

Positive

Information can be available almost instantly; less expensive than a personal interview ($20 to $90 per interview); fast; low chance of question misinterpretation; high response rate (up to 85 percent); you control who responds.

Negative

Limited to short interviews; response rate can be as low as 20 percent; bias between interviewer and respondent; not everyone you need to reach may have a phone; not everyone you need to reach will be willing to talk.

Personal Interview

Positive

Flexible, in that you control the direction of the interview; extensive information can be obtained; visual aids can be used; high response rate (70 percent to 90 percent); you control who actually responds.

Negative

Most expensive ($150 to $400 per interview); there could be bias between interviewer and respondent; refusal rate could be high; very rich or very poor are hard to reach.

How many people to interview is a different question and depends entirely on your personal situation, i.e., what your product is and the market segment you are targeting. The trick is to make sure you aren't getting biased responses to your questions. In the words of the industry, you need to give all of your potential customers an equal chance of being interviewed and you want to communicate with enough of them to be certain that they are truly a representative sample of the entire segment. Talking to a handful of potential customers won't give you sufficient information to decide whether you have developed a product they will want.

I've had clients who have sampled all the people who stopped at their trade booths at a trade show. Again, that information may be useful, but it is also biased because a certain type of person shows up at trade booths and they do not necessarily represent the broader population to whom you are trying to sell.

So what can you do? The answer depends on how serious you are about making certain you can generalize your survey questions to the entire group you are targeting. If you are serious, then there's no substitute for bringing in a smart survey research professional to help you figure out what sample size you need to be truly legitimate and to assist you in finding those people who will make up the sample.

On the other hand, if you are more interested in simply gauging whether you are on the right track, I've found that a truly random (i.e., no friends, relatives, known business associates, golf partners, support group members, etc.) selection of 100 possible customers is very useful. The choice is yours. If you can afford it, find a survey researcher; if not, track down those 100 people yourself. Let's go back to the three types of interviews and review them in detail.

Mail Interviews

Mailed questionnaires are usually the least expensive method of collecting information from your market. You develop a list of questions; send them to your sample, and analyze their responses as they are returned. I always write a personal cover letter to accompany the survey and explain its purpose. Hopefully, it also motivates the reader to answer the questions. The questionnaire is an opportunity to make a positive first impression on potential customers before they are approached as buyers of the product. Basically, the following information needs to be covered in the letter:

What this survey is about

Why the respondent is important

A promise of confidentiality

A promise of a copy of results

A way for the respondent to contact you with questions

How to get results back to you

A thank you

Always use your letterhead, and personally sign the letters. I also use first class mail because it suggests the importance of the survey to me. I have even been known to use certified or special delivery letters when I want to communicate a sense of urgency to the prospect. (See example on the next page.)

There are also some fairly basic ground rules for questionnaires.

They need to be short enough so that people will take the time to respond. (I try to stick to less than 50 questions.)

The questions themselves need to be brief, and you should start with an easy question. For example, "Do you buy diapers?"

Simple wording should be used; for example, don't use the word "assistance" when you can say "help" or "priority" when you can use "most important."

Be specific.

Be careful to avoid questions that could be objectionable, such as, "Why haven't you ever hired Hispanics?"

Don't ask for opinions unless you really need them. People tend not to communicate opinions well in writing, which makes it difficult to figure out what they are really trying to say to you.

Give specific directions on how to answer questions. Example: "Please check the appropriate box."

And finally, use closed-ended questions. These are the type where there is only one possible answer, and you've listed all the choices right on the questionnaire.

Example: Closed-Ended Question

What is your age? Please check one:

[   ] Under 16
[   ] 16-21
[   ] 22-30
[   ] 31-40
[   ] 41-50
[   ] 51-60
[   ] Over 60

An open-ended question does not have obvious choices. An example would be, "How can New York improve its school system?" As you can see, the possible responses are numerous and are a real headache to categorize. Don't use open-ended questions unless you absolutely must.

Example: Cover Letter

August 5, 1991

Mr. John Smith
123 Main Street
Ann Arbor, MI 48104

Dear Mr. Smith:

Debbie's Diapers is in the business of exporting cotton diapers from China. As we plan for 1993, we would appreciate your views as a user of more than 10,000 diapers per month in your diaper service. Your input will help us to decide how many diapers to order this year as well as which sizes, colors, and styles to focus on.

The enclosed survey takes approximately five minutes to complete, and all responses are kept in total confidence. I also would be delighted to send you a copy of our survey results for your own use. Simply enclose a note with your name and address along with the questionnaire.

We have enclosed a self-addressed, stamped envelope for the completed questionnaire. Thank you for taking the time to help us develop a product line that truly meets the needs of our customers.

Sincerely,

Debbie Dunlop
President

Example: Customer Survey

Please check the appropriate box for each question, and return the survey as soon as possible in the enclosed self-addressed, stamped envelope. We also welcome any additional comments you may have and have provided space for such at the end of the questionnaire. Thank you for your time.

1. Do you own a personal computer?   ❏ Yes   ❏ No

2. Is it an IBM compatible?   ❏ Yes   ❏ No

3. Is it an Apple computer?   ❏ Yes   ❏ No

4. How often do you use it? Please check the one most appropriate answer.

    ❏ Less than monthly

    ❏ Less than once per week

    ❏ Less than once per week

    ❏ Daily

5. Have you begun to do any retirement planning?   ❏ Yes   ❏ No

6. Are you using an adviser for retirement planning?   ❏ Yes   ❏ No

7. If yes, who are you using? Please check all that apply.

    ❏ Financial planner

    ❏ Banker

    ❏ Accountant

    ❏ Stock Broker

    ❏ Attorney

    ❏ Insurance Agent

    ❏ Other _____

8. If you have not begun to do planning, are you thinking about starting to do some?

❏ Yes—Why?_____

❏ No—Why?_____

9. Are you interested in a software tutorial that could teach you the concepts of planning?

    ❏ Yes—Why?_____

❑ No—Why? _____

10. Are you interested in a software program that helps you to plan?

 ❑ Yes—Why?_____

 ❑ No—Why? _____

11. Are you interested in software that teaches the concepts and helps you to plan?

 ❑ Yes—Why?_____

 ❑ No—Why? _____

12. If you are interested in any of the types of software listed above, how much would you consider paying for each?

Tutorial Software	Planning Software	Tutorial and Planning Software
❑ Under $50	❑ Under $50	❑ Under $50
❑ $50–100	❑ $50–100	❑ $50–100
❑ $100–150	❑ $100–150	❑ $100–150
❑ $150–200	❑ $150–200	❑ $150–200
❑ Over $200	❑ Over $200	❑ Over $200

13. If you purchase software, where do you normally buy it?

 ❐ Computer store

 ❐ Retail store

 ❐ Mail order

 ❐ User's club

 ❐ Other _____

14. If you purchase software, where do you find out about it?

 ❐ Friends/family

 ❐ Business associates

 ❐ Retail store

 ❐ Computer store

 ❐ User's club

 ❐ Television

❐ Computer network

❐ Newspaper

❐ Other _____

Please let us know a little about you.

What is your sex?   ❑ Male   ❑ Female

What is your age?

❐ Over 65

❐ 61–65

❐ 51–60

❐ 35–50

❐ 22-34

❐ 13–21

❐ 7–12

❐ 2–6

❐ 0–1

What is your income level?

❐ Under $5,000

❐ $5,000–9,999

❐ $10,000–14,999

❐ $15,000–29,999

❐ $30,000–49,999

❐ $50,000–69,999

❐ $70,000–99,999

❐ $100,000 or over

What is your educational level?

❐ Some high school

❐ Some college

❐ Associate's Degree

❒ Bachelor's Degree

❒ Some graduate school

❒ Advanced degree

❒ What is your profession?

❒ Homemaker

❒ Student

❒ Self-employed

❒ Service

❒ Retail

❒ Manufacturing

❒ Please add any additional comments here:

_____

_____

_____

_____

_____

Always, always pretest a questionnaire. In other words, try it out on a few people first to see if it works before you actually take it to the streets. This will tell you:

+ if anyone will even answer the questions;

+ if the questions are understood;

+ if the questions are interpreted in basically the same way;

+ if they answer the actual questions;

+ if they answer the questions in a way that is so confusing to you that they are meaningless;

+ if they don't like some part of the questionnaire (or worse, all of it); and,

+ if they thought you were leading them too much, i.e., trying to get them to answer one way or another.

Once you have done a pretest that indicates you have a survey people will answer, mail it out.

Again, there are lots of rules on how, when and why to mail and many, many books on the subject should you want more detailed information on surveys. Your main concern at this point is to get those surveys returned. In my experience, there are some obvious tasks that will help to increase your chances of success.

Make certain you have the right address and the correct spelling of the respondent's name.

If you aren't sure about the address, pay enough postage so that the questionnaire is returned to you if it is incorrect.

Send personalized envelopes so that people don't think that they have another piece of junk mail to throw away.

Be clear about who should complete the survey. (I do that by sending the survey to the specific person, even if it takes me more time and expense to find him.)

Don't forget to enclose the self-addressed, postage-paid envelope. I cringe to think how often I've forgotten this.

Once you have mailed out the questionnaires, what can you expect? There should be an initial surge of responses from people like me who compulsively fill out every questionnaire mailed to them. Beyond that, you should probably send a reminder post card to respondents about two weeks after the initial mailing.

Example: Postcard Reminder

For the stragglers, you may need to send a new questionnaire and cover letter three to four weeks later. People who haven't responded within a month won't. That leaves you with the task of analyzing the questionnaires, which is a fairly straight-forward process. Basically, you tabulate the responses, constantly asking yourself, "What is this telling me about my customers; what is this telling me about how and what I should sell to them?" At best, it will confirm your identification of the market, telling you that you have indeed identified a niche or segment that wants your product. At worst, you'll discover that you've identified the wrong segment and need to rethink who your customers will be or that you need to rethink your product.

July 4, 1992

Two weeks ago a questionnaire was sent to you asking about
_____. If you have already completed the survey and
mailed it back to me, thank you. If you haven't, please take the
time to fill it out and mail it today. Your opinions mean a great
deal to XYZ Company because they will help us to design our
product.

If you did not receive our survey for some reason, please call Susan
Smith at 800-555-5555, toll free, and we will send another to you
immediately.

Thank you for your time.

S. Larkin, President
XYZ Co.
503 East 4th Street

Telephone Interviews

When mailing will take too long or you want to increase the number of
respondents to your questionnaire, telephone interviews are in order.
Some marketing professionals refer to this as telemarketing, although I
think of telemarketing more as actually calling people to sell the product.
With phone surveys, you still need to select a sample carefully to make
sure it is random and really does reflect your market segment. Telephone
interviews can be difficult because they depend entirely on verbal instead
of visual communication: there is more room for misinterpretation on the
part of the respondent. There is also more room for bias in the responses
in that they may be more positive if they like the sound of the
interviewer's voice or more negative if they don't. And, you need to be
careful to write down exactly every single item you want the interviewer
to say or do during the call, or you'll create more bias.

I always mail a letter to the people who will be interviewed just to
forewarn them that a phone call is coming their way.

After letters are sent, I organize cover sheets for the interviews, and
prepare the questionnaires for interviewers. A typical cover sheet might
look like the following.

Example: Telephone Survey Pre-mailing

August 5, 1991

Mr. Joe Smith
123 Main Street
Ann Arbor, MI 48104

Dear Mr. Smith:

I am writing to ask you for your help with a marketing study I am doing for my business.

About a year ago, I purchased 350 acres in Onedaga County to develop a retreat center, primarily for recovering alcoholics. The main focus of the center will be a 30-person lodge providing a peaceful, natural setting for groups and individuals alike. Groups will be welcome to use the center for their own purposes, and individuals will be invited to use the lodge as a place of retreat.

The cost of staying at the center will range from $150 for the day use of a conference room and $120 for an overnight stay including dinner and breakfast, to $370 for a full weekend retreat for an individual.

I have asked Jamie Markus, Ph.D., to call you for your feedback. My biggest question is whether or not there is a market large enough to support this type of center.

I look forward to your feedback, and thank you in advance for your help.

Sincerely,

Sarth Larkin
President

Example: Interview Cover Sheet

NAME:_____

PHONE NUMBER: _____

STREET:_____

CITY: _____

DATE	TIME	INTERVIEWER	RESULT	RECALLS NEEDED

I then contact each person's home or office (whichever is appropriate) to do the interview or set up a time when it will be more convenient to do so.

Each interviewer also needs a list of questions and problems that may come up from respondents so that they'll know how to react if such things arise. Most of the following list of reasons for refusals is taken from *Mail and Telephone Surveys: Total Design Method* by Don Dillman and offers fairly typical examples of the kinds of refusals you may be able to turn into interviews.

Example: Possible Answers to Reasons for Refusals

Reason For Refusing	.. And Possible Responses
Too busy	This should only take (the number of) minutes. I would be happy to call back if I've called you at a bad time. When is the best time for me to call in the next several days?
Bad health	I'm sorry to hear that. Would that be okay to call back in several days?
Too old or too young (be reasonable here. You don't want children answering your survey unless your product is for them)	Older (younger) people's opinions are just as important in this particular survey as anyone else's. In order for the results to be representative, we have to be sure everyone has a chance to give their opinion.
Don't know enough to answer	Our questions are pretty easy. I'll just read a few to you, and you can see what they are like.
Not interested	It's important that we get to everyone in our sample, otherwise our results won't help us. I'd really like to talk with you.
No one else's business what I think	I certainly understand. We're just trying to get a sense of how we can best serve our clients.
Objects to surveys	I understand (and don't like surveys much myself). We think this particular survey is very important because it will tell us how to best serve our clients. We would really like to have your opinion.
Objects to telephone surveys	We just recently have started doing our surveys by telephone, because this way saves time for our respondents.

When it is time to do the survey, interviewers usually need to be reminded to write down the date and time of the interview, and to read questions exactly as they've been written. Sometimes it is worth putting together a rule book.

Typical rules include marking the time the interview starts, reading questions precisely as written, and using neutral probes such as "Yes, I see" stated in an expectant manner.

Personal Interviews

Face-to-face surveys are wonderful if you can get people to talk with you. I have learned that the key to getting an interview is to offer some information that is useful to the respondent first and then to ask for some of his or her time. For example, I have had good luck when I have offered to share results of industry surveys or competitive analyses that they want at the same meeting.

Face-to-face interviews always need an introductory letter similar to one you would send regarding telephone interviews. I actually use personal interviews in combination with a mailed questionnaire when I want to delve into an area more deeply. Once I've received mailed questionnaire responses, I write down issues or questions that are raised and develop a leaner survey, usually with no more than twenty questions. I then make a list of key potential customers or choose a random subset of my original sample, and send them a letter asking for no more than a half hour of time. Yes, interviews sometimes take longer than that, but I try hard to let that be the choice of the person being interviewed. I always end a question with, "Is there anything else you would like to add?" or an equivalent phrase when I do face-to-face interviews.

For each type of interview—mail, telephone, or personal—always send a personal thank you to respondents for their time.

Focus Groups

There are times when pulling together a group of people at the same time can be very useful. The reason for this is that the individuals feed off of each other in terms of opinions, ideas, and feedback. Focus groups, which are groups of eight to sixteen people, provide you with this depth of feedback. There are many rules about focus groups:

They should be a part of your identified market segment.

They should not be your friends.

They should be selected as randomly as possible.

They should be interviewed in a neutral place (not your office and not theirs).

They should not be interviewed by you personally because they may not want to tell you negative things (and you need to know what the negatives are).

Potential focus group members usually are invited to the group through the use of a personal letter.

Unlike other types of interviews, focus group questions tend to be open-ended once the interviewer has a sense of who the group members are. Normally, everyone sits around a table and is asked to introduce themselves by name and to say a little bit about their company or the use of products similar to the one in question. The interviewer also introduces herself and tells the group what the goal of the meeting is. (Example: To learn about ABC product, what you like about it, what you don't like, whether you would buy it and where, and how much you would spend.) She also describes the process, which is usually a series of questions asked with responses recorded on cassette or video, and estimates the amount of time the session will take.

Most focus groups run between one and two hours. Refreshments containing caffeine and sugar are almost always provided (to make sure the group is lively). A typical set of questions might look like the following list. These are aimed at assessing the effectiveness of a program aimed at women in transition on the East Coast.

Example: Focus Group Questions

Introduction: As you may know, the Women's Life Center (WLC) opened in 1985 with the goal of helping women to take control of their own lives. Help comes in the form of:

✦ Counseling

✦ Support groups

Example: Focus Group Letter

December 28, 1991

Ms. Agnes Jones
154 State Street
Chicago, IL 60611

Dear Ms. Jones:

I am working with the Chicago Art Association to develop a long term plan and need your help. Much of what the Association does in the future will depend on its past activities and the needs of its clients.

With this letter I would like to invite you to be my guest for lunch at Grif's Grill on North Saginaw at noon on January 16, 1992. I've asked ten people to join us to talk about the association, what it does well, where improvements could be made, and what you think its goals should be going into 1993.

I will telephone you next week to see if you can join us. I hope you can. Thank you.

Best regards,

Geri Larkin, Ph.D.
/lp

- ✦ Information and referral assistance
- ✦ Child care
- ✦ Emergency housing

The center has really grown since it started in 1977. The purpose of this luncheon is simply to get some feedback from you regarding its work.

1. When did you first find out about the center? (You want the date and the situatiuon the person was in.)
2. What did you think the center was?
3. What services did it provide?
4. Has it changed over time?
5. How has it changed (programs, staff, clients, bigger/smaller)?
6. Is it better or worse than it was when you first learned about it?
7. Why is it better/worse?
8. Have you used any of the programs of the center? If yes, which?

   What did you like?

   What didn't you like?
9. How do you think the center should move into the 1990s?

   Should the programs change? How?

   Should the staff change? How?
10. What is your vision for the center five years from now (the year 2000)?
11. How about ten years from now?
12. Anything else?

THANK YOU.

U sing Professionals

Unless you have done surveys and focus groups before, it is a good idea to find a research organization capable of developing a questionnaire for you, selecting your interview sample, doing the survey (or showing you how to do it), and analyzing the results for you.

Most major universities have staff who can do surveys. Call a marketing professor in the business school, or the statistics department, or the survey research department if one exists. Brace yourself for the cost. A good survey can cost more than $10,000. To save money, do as much front work as you can by yourself. If you can't find a university professor who can help, ask your lawyer, banker, accountant, or other professional contacts for suggestions. They should come up with someone who is reputable. Another source is the American Association of Public Opinion Research (AAPOR). They can be contacted at P.O. Box 17, Princeton, N.J.

Remember that we all have fairly well-defined patterns of buying behavior that can be discovered through surveys. We usually buy products in some predictable way. Video movies are usually rented on weekends, tutors are most often hired three to four weeks before exam time; office supplies usually are ordered monthly. And we can be very loyal. Once customers start buying a product, they want to stay with it. Do you still purchase a particular shampoo even though you know there are new brands emerging all the time? My family replaces Chryslers with Chryslers; companies who start with Apple products usually stay with Apple products.

At the same time, we can be influenced by the media, colleagues, and opinions in our own industries. A smart marketer always will figure out what ultimately influences the buying patterns of potential customers. The media, for example, has many of us drinking wine coolers these days, a product that didn't even exist several years ago.

As you draw a picture of who your customers are, use interviews to figure out what they really want. Find out how sensitive your market is to price changes and changes in how you might decide to sell your product, i.e. directly or through some other distribution system. Find out what product they want the most. In other words, find out from your customers what they want you to sell to them and how they want you to sell it.

Finding Your Customers
for Feedback

Techniques for Finding the Customers You've Defined

Now that you know the questions you want to ask, how do you find the people to ask? This is your eighth step, finding and surveying your customers. If you are already in business, then you know who your customers are, at least for now. You will still want to survey them on a regular basis, using the techniques described in Chapter Seven to make sure you aren't side-tracked by surprises in their product preferences.

If you are starting a business, or a new product line, finding people or companies to survey becomes a more difficult task. Fortunately, census and other information can help.

Where should you start? If you are selling to people you can take the customer profile you have developed and start asking your friends and acquaintances if they, or someone they know, fit your profile. Once you start identifying customers in this way, you can start asking them about their own behavior patterns—associations they have, magazines or newspapers to which they have subscriptions, etc. Their responses will give you clues regarding places where you will be able to find more potential customers. For example, if you are selling a special aftermarket sports headlight for cars, you may discover that your potential customers will attend a specific car rally every year and are avid readers of *Hot Rod Magazine.* Knowing that, you can set up a booth at the rally to interview potential customers or purchase a list of all the subscribers to the magazine in your geographical market. Those subscribers can then be surveyed.

The process for locating companies who are potential customers takes some basic library research. After profiling companies who would be potential customers, you can find companies fitting those parameters in a number of directories. My favorite is Dun & Bradstreet's *Million Dollar Directory,* because it is organized geographically and includes information such as revenues, number of employees, main product line, officers, address, telephone number, bank, and accountant used. For smaller companies, Chamber of Commerce membership lists can be very effective and are often free or inexpensive for market researchers.

Mailing Lists

I have found mailing lists to be invaluable as well, although I've mostly used them for finding people instead of companies. Basically, a mailing list is a compilation of the names, addresses and telephone numbers for individuals and companies broken down by certain characteristics. You can order a list according to characteristics such as income level, sex, home address, magazine subscriptions, memberships, etc. The larger mailing list companies have up to 100 million names on file and are constantly updating those names so that you get current information. And most firms will sell you anything from labels to non-magnetic tapes to 3 x 5 inch cards to diskettes. Prices start at approximately $40 per thousand names, and there is usually a minimum order.

A Sample of Mailing List Categories

Advertising Agencies	Accountants
Affluent Americans	Air Pollution Controllers
Animal Hospitals	Architects
Art Schools	Athletic Coaches
Automotive	Banks
Barber Shops	Beer/Liquor Stores
Blue Collar workers	Book Buyers
Bookstores	Boy Scouts
Cafes	Catholic High Schools
Child Psychiatrists	Churches
Civil Engineers	Clinics
Chambers of Commerce	Clubs
Colleges	Computer Engineers
Contractors	Contributors
Corporations	Counselors
Dance Studios	Detectives
Doctors	Durable Goods Wholesalers
Drillers	Editors
Educators	Electric Appliances
Electroplaters	Elementary Teachers
Engineers	Environmental Researchers
Executives	Families
Farmers	Female Military Personnel
Food Stores	Furniture Stores
Galleries	Game Retailers
Gourmet Food Buyers	Government Officials
Grandparents	Gun Dealers
Halls	Helicopter Owners

Hobbies/Crafts
Hospitals
Hypnotists
Industrial Designers
Investors
Joggers
Junk/Scrap Dealers
Labor Unions
Libraries
Machine Shops
Mail Order Buyers
Middle Managers
Mutual Savings Bonds
Nurses
Orphanages
Personnel Agencies
Photographers
Pilots
Presidents, Women's Clubs
Public Libraries
Quakers
Radio Stations
Religious Contributors
Rubbish Removal
Schools
Senior Citizen Organizations
Sororities
Steel Executives
Summer Camps
Tax Attorneys
Teenagers
Therapists
Travel Agents
Unions
Vacation Resorts
Veterinarians
Waste Paper Dealers

Women Ad Agencies
YMCAs

Homeowners
Hotels
Ice Cream Stores
Insurance Agents
Jails
Judges
Kindergartens
Laundries
Limousine Services
Magazine Subscribers
Manufacturers
Musicians
Newspaper Publishers
Offices
Paint Shops
Pet Shops
Physicists
Pizza Restaurants
Prominent Women
Purchasing Executives
Rabbis
Real Estate Agents
Residents Household
Saddlery Dealers
Scientists
Soap Manufacturers
Sporting Good Wholesalers
Stock Brokers
Surfboard Stores
Teachers
Tennis Players
Toy Manufacturers
Truck Drivers
Utilities
Vegetable/Fruit Sellers
Volunteer Fire Departments
Who's Prominent in art, banking, etc.

Zoos

THE JET SET
(America's Most Wealthy)

	Highest Salaried Execs at Home Address	Social Register	Prominent Medical Specialists	Attorneys	Wealthy at Home	Prominent Americans	Yacht Owners 38'+	Wealthy Women	Corporation Presidents at Business Address	Aircraft Owners
ALABAMA	593	57	6,526	5,279	41,512	1,450	746	4,796	3,917	1,899
ALASKA	44	8	826	1,769	27,109	283	2,518	1,270	648	6,134
ARIZONA	435	204	7,402	6,986	45,921	1,733	295	4,176	4,034	3,998
ARKANSAS	304	9	3,554	4,004	20,667	622	139	1,851	2,273	1,580
CALIFORNIA	3,957	2,199	64,910	77,286	465,174	12,871	16,964	40,800	21,520	23,808
COLORADO	713	280	7,028	11,276	84,542	2,262	228	8,240	4,432	3,236
CONNECTICUT	2,843	1,896	9,225	8,840	63,907	3,364	2,613	7,865	6,279	1,457
DELAWARE	156	173	1,402	1,250	11,804	433	558	752	5,489	568
DIST. COLUMBIA	133	706	4,405	12,319	11,875	2,172	392	2,532	4	164
FLORIDA	1,874	1,399	24,949	28,533	301,142	5,006	11,505	26,999	10,825	8,670
GEORGIA	1,137	200	10,500	13,768	83,809	2,540	1,079	10,099	5,124	3,562
HAWAII	163	46	2,524	2,822	14,579	519	630	1,630	1,972	307
IDAHO	150	29	1,437	1,685	15,799	344	77	1,288	1,173	1,544
ILLINOIS	4,173	838	25,049	37,347	134,127	7,356	2,791	11,569	19,382	5,562
INDIANA	1,406	76	8,946	10,508	55,995	2,377	676	5,118	8,718	2,817
IOWA	624	9	5,134	6,668	33,081	1,183	308	3,528	4,527	1,804
KANSAS	703	11	4,743	5,758	35,702	1,337	104	4,358	3,727	2,313
KENTUCKY	552	74	6,264	8,438	26,501	912	566	2,684	3,868	1,180
LOUISIANA	518	116	8,207	12,122	51,180	1,345	2,037	4,764	3,937	1,771
MAINE	277	365	2,497	2,320	19,401	518	1,534	1,485	1,534	1,065
MARYLAND	1,183	1,409	13,654	9,289	88,740	3,836	5,035	10,361	2,417	2,055
MASSACHUSETTS	2,758	2,663	18,876	21,125	130,771	4,424	4,524	18,382	5,991	2,699
MICHIGAN	1,921	115	20,465	17,575	129,273	3,373	6,219	7,960	14,132	5,545
MINNESOTA	1,261	65	9,466	12,343	61,041	2,146	991	4,497	8,098	3,590
MISSISSIPPI	265	17	3,412	4,427	20,358	609	482	1,241	2,394	1,196
MISSOURI	1,234	652	11,045	12,802	59,141	2,463	451	5,754	11,699	3,125
MONTANA	75	22	1,312	1,797	11,784	268	25	865	966	1,602
NEBRASKA	415	14	3,067	3,311	19,486	622	2,094	2,094	2,601	1,286
NEVADA	118	22	1,764	2,278	17,365	336	254	1,845	1,023	1,759
NEW HAMPSHIRE	413	318	2,198	1,798	22,644	613	564	2,353	2,054	1,349
NEW JERSEY	4,054	1,028	19,075	21,079	119,565	4,644	3,752	13,482	10,550	2,720
NEW MEXICO	123	89	2,884	3,188	20,964	1,068	50	2,937	1,735	1,668
NEW YORK	5,990	5,011	54,237	65,973	273,262	15,074	7,147	55,732	10,593	4,698
NO. CAROLINA	1,229	216	11,650	9,745	86,512	2,456	1,273	7,773	5,158	3,344
NORTH DAKOTA	94	0	1,357	924	8,393	209	21	558	666	1,040
OHIO	3,585	741	22,693	27,773	148,867	5,032	3,119	20,353	18,937	5,544
OKLAHOMA	559	15	5,908	8,611	35,538	1,268	202	2,720	6,819	2,879
OREGON	360	79	6,143	6,336	42,720	1,030	1,491	4,344	6,075	3,900
PENNSYLVANIA	3,773	3,580	30,745	20,053	152,713	5,202	3,031	14,162	18,267	4,515
RHODE ISLAND	397	255	2,610	1,213	17,407	517	891	2,036	2,510	302
SO. CAROLINA	473	257	5,713	4,834	44,859	1,268	607	3,565	2,653	1,300
SOUTH DAKOTA	87	2	1,151	982	7,483	256	22	538	862	930
TENNESSEE	822	76	9,343	10,764	49,293	1,740	769	4,284	4,557	2,256
TEXAS	3,447	401	28,794	35,975	238,553	6,979	2,667	34,582	19,292	12,524
UTAH	265	19	3,276	3,380	19,983	775	101	1,340	2,409	1,036
VERMONT	171	252	1,347	1,375	9,551	395	191	1,155	1,003	452
VIRGINIA	1,352	810	11,821	14,772	104,397	4,415	3,185	11,285	3,330	2,412
WASHINGTON	632	132	9,376	11,532	92,027	1,711	6,613	6,600	2,432	5,262
WEST VIRGINIA	240	13	3,844	3,009	12,558	457	105	1,193	993	757
WISCONSIN	1,526	53	9,555	11,791	63,686	2,108	1,068	5,832	9,184	2,932
WYOMING	64	41	802	948	8,044	259	18	907	554	681
TOTALS	59,641	27,016	540,824	610,610	3,664,318	124,226	100,774	396,774	300,017	216,021

NEW! MEDICAL DOCTORS
(By Specialty)

PRIMARY SPECIALTIES	TOTAL U.S. MDs	OFFICE BASED TOTAL	HOSPITAL BASED 1st YEAR RESI-DENTS	OTHER RESI-DENTS	STAFF
Adolescent Medicine	1,102	751	1	55	121
Aeorspace Medicine	792	382	2	36	187
Allergy	1,934	1,732	3	60	46
Allergy and Immunology	1,322	1,117		33	51
Anesthesiology	21,262	12,277	432	3,942	2,742
Blood Banking	239	127		9	36
Cardiovascular Diseases	11,518	8,533	1	653	1,168
Critical Care	444	238		36	102
Dermatology	7,334	5,944	66	647	263
Dermatopathology	153	132		6	9
Diabetes	616	450	1	6	49
Emergency Medicine	13,364	5,763	436	1,621	4,278
Endocrinology	1,851	1,205	1	73	215
Endocrinology, Reproductive	378	288	2	17	36
Family Practice	59,891	44,002	2,034	8,619	1,951
Gastroenterology	5,323	4,145	8	261	394
General Practice	24,504	19,705	30	1,471	1,547
General Preventive Medicine	1,975	851	1	491	178
Genetics	372	196		13	77
Geriatrics	1,013	544	3	40	189
Gynecology	4,680	4,181	1	52	169
Hematology	1,700	943	1	113	292
Immunology	307	157		24	29
Immunology, Diagnostic Lab	117	105		1	5
Immunopathology	125	107		1	7
Infectious Diseases	1,835	855	4	147	356
Internal Medicine	81,074	42,494	4,945	21,469	5,465
Legal Medicine	346	237		4	20
Maternal and Fetal Medicine	327	192		19	63
Neonatal-Perinatal Medicine	1,495	702	6	96	430
Nephrology	2,335	1,589	2	112	327
Neurology	7,372	4,503	100	1,111	869
Neurology, Child	748	399	2	58	154
Neuropathology	255	153	1	13	50
Nuclear Medicine	1,107	525		89	355
Nutrition	262	208		10	9
Obstetrics	834	633	3	92	50
Obstetrics and Gynecology	25,545	17,489	1,172	4,514	1,102
Occupational and Industrial Medicine	2,793	1,461	1	79	205
Oncology	3,400	2,282	4	197	458
Oncology, Gynecology	531	383		34	59
Ophthalmology	15,078	12,097	160	1,698	442
Otology	627	516	2	27	22
Otorhinolaryngology	7,133	5,521	126	882	302
Pathology	10,177	3,578	338	1,787	3,131

Table continues

STATE	TOTAL U.S. MDs
ALABAMA	6,526
ALASKA	826
ARIZONA	7,402
ARKANSAS	3,554
CALIFORNIA	64,910
COLORADO	7,028
CONNECTICUT	9,225
DELAWARE	1,402
DIST. COLUMBIA	4,405
FLORIDA	24,949
GEORGIA	10,500
HAWAII	2,524
IDAHO	1,437
ILLINOIS	25,049
INDIANA	8,946
IOWA	5,134
KANSAS	4,743
KENTUCKY	6,264
LOUISIANA	8,207
MAINE	2,497
MARYLAND	13,654
MASSACHUSETTS	18,876
MICHIGAN	20,465
MINNESOTA	9,466
MISSISSIPPI	3,412
MISSOURI	11,145
MONTANA	1,312
NEGBRASKA	3,067
NEVADA	1,764
NEW HAMPSHIRE	2,198
NEW JERSEY	19,075
NEW MEXICO	2,884
NEW YORK	54,237
NO. CAROLINA	11,650
NORTH DAKOTA	1,357
OHIO	22,694
OKLAHOMA	5,908

Table continues

NEW! MEDICAL DOCTORS
(By Specialty)

PRIMARY SPECIALTIES	TOTAL U.S. MDs	OFFICE BASED TOTAL	HOSPITAL BASED 1st YEAR RESI- DENTS	OTHER RESI- DENTS	STAFF
Pathology, Anatomic	1,640	662	12	133	636
Pathology, Chemical	199	137		6	28
Pathology, Clinical	777	305	4	57	275
Pathology, Forensic	377	233	1	11	41
Pathology, Radioisotopic	141	123		4	10
Pediatrics	35,912	19,873	1,998	7,274	2,847
Pediatrics, Allergy	290	237	1	11	18
Pediatrics, Cardiology	701	408		44	143
Pediatrics, Endocrinology	366	195		12	76
Pediatrics, Hematology-Oncology	653	292		31	169
Pediatrics, Nephrology	279	149		8	63
Pharmacology, Clinical	409	192		12	36
Physical Medicine and Rehabilitation	3,729	1,893	140	809	618
Psychiatry	32,841	18,406	1,068	4,821	5,188
Psychiatry, Child	2,786	1,657	11	274	446
Psychoanalysis/Psych Hypnosis	983	920	1	8	19
Public Medicine	1,200	290	10	44	55
Pulmonary Diseases	3,784	2,691	9	168	406
Radiology	10,05	5,689	19	1,562	1,833
Radiology, Diagnostic	10,183	6,246	443	1,695	1,323
Radiology, Nuclear	200	151		13	26
Radilology, Pediatric	285	190		5	75
Radiology, Therapeutic	2,240	1,423	29	411	297
Rheumatology	2,210	1,653	2	74	190
Surgery, Addominal	304	6,249		12	25
Surgery, Cardiovascular	2,096	1,640	3	142	191
Surgery, Colon and Rectal	936	840	2	18	33
Surgery, General	31,937	18,183	1,870	8,236	1,834
Surgery, Hand	666	583		15	26
Surgery, Head and Neck	717	466	4	170	38
Surgery, Maxillofacial	349	237	2	78	12
Surgery, Neurological	3,886	2,652	57	628	284
Surgery, Orthopedic	17,572	12,551	541	3,021	750
Surgery, Pediatric	557	418	2	19	65
Surgery, Plastic	3,862	3,255	16	294	137
Surgery, Thoracic	1,549	1,156	4	88	166
Surgery, Traumatic	241	165		7	38
Surgery, Urological	8,801	6,908	125	975	394
Surgery, Vascular	1,132	935	3	31	99
Flexible Residency Program	2,215	130	1,012	1,062	5
Other Specialty	4,489	1,762	239	728	516
Unspecified Specialty	18,508	9,453	5	1,281	665
TOTALS	**540,824**	**335,292**	**18,747**	**86,900**	**48,121**

STATE	TOTAL U.S. MDs
OREGON	6,143
PENNSYLVANIA	30,745
PUERTO RICO	3,943
RHODE ISLAND	2,610
SO. CAROLINA	5,713
SOUTH DAKOTA	1,151
TENNESSEE	9,343
TEXAS	28,794
UTAH	3,276
VERMONT	1,347
VIRGINIA	11,821
VIRGIN ISLANDS	175
WASHINGTON	9,375
WEST VIRGINIA	3,844
WISCONSIN	9,555
WYOMING	802
PACIFIC ISLANDS	186
APO/FPO, FOREIGN	109
GRAND TOTALS	**540,824**

5,000 minimum

HEADS OF HOUSEHOLD BY AGE*

	18-34	35-54	55-64	65+	Households with a Child	Homeowners Residing 5 Years
ALABAMA	303,694	623,399	142,183	185,733	221,864	447,968
ALASKA	21,096	28,321	5,228	3,647	9,344	24,321
ARAIZONA	204,489	651,154	198,239	228,726	194,747	361,815
ARKANSAS	52,346	289,748	186,077	149,760	124,584	237,372
CALIFORNIA	2,428,952	4,526,962	1,077,211	1,368,604	1,405,901	2,557,897
COLORADO	339,551	616,076	161,608	182,706	196,985	396,037
CONNECTICUT	114,311	494,350	140,171	156,514	159,240	390,402
DELAWARE	61,531	115,475	37,666	38,252	42,774	83,776
DIST. COLUMBIA	61,071	97,057	29,391	36,707	19,074	45,360
FLORIDA	944,174	2,258,795	834,623	1,124,880	524,193	1,283,167
GEORGIA	338,991	541,288	159,986	199,007	243,761	557,421
HAWAII	74,060	92,781	27,771	28,749	31,004	63,033
IDAHO	82,426	164,517	42,302	59,172	63,038	124,949
ILLINOIS	897,534	1,875,247	595,630	726,025	810,645	1,486,248
INDIANA	193,597	725,536	228,859	248,647	299,426	716,613
IOWA	246,332	458,695	146,530	244,583	210,632	487,932
KANSAS	157,051	297,533	94,979	143,913	136,820	354,411
KENTUCKY	214,511	567,210	154,241	174,266	207,580	419,080
LOUISIANA	295,673	672,203	210,443	220,074	254,928	541,458
MAINE	84,074	208,656	54,550	63,550	60,066	112,503
MARYLAND	192,923	554,392	174,881	203,243	204,193	435,442
MASSACHUSETTS	567,006	1,039,307	326,376	416,670	351,795	761,027
MICHIGAN	756,949	1,454,649	489,173	607,866	648,362	1,346,231
MINNESOTA	401,461	709,583	215,397	290,850	318,261	639,023
MISSISSIPPI	154,866	375,347	109,464	122,969	122,050	279,344
MISSOURI	417,057	835,004	276,543	360,415	348,190	723,941
MONTANA	77,760	107,129	27,074	37,853	41,952	101,889
NEBRASKA	155,076	237,787	70,094	103,897	123,186	272,174
NEVADA	117,132	202,372	59,804	58,473	55,848	87,942
NEW HAMPSHIRE	75,733	224,083	42,705	43,997	54,011	98,955
NEW JERSEY	325,241	807,403	270,230	320,624	312,636	781,277
NEW MEXICO	102,634	101,382	29,051	45,252	48,569	121,089
NEW YORK	1,196,688	2,691,908	884,667	1,107,017	952,044	1,642,022
NORTH CAROLINA	479,451	1,120,997	310,927	302,532	414,928	877,437
NORTH DAKOTA	46,797	95,161	31,893	48,022	49,452	101,870
OHIO	865,661	1,697,405	586,394	772,861	828,166	1,604,210
OKLAHOMA	134,229	310,293	111,301	136,033	124,503	359,565
OREGON	159,112	293,917	100,388	165,090	112,141	294,218
PENNSYLVANIA	447,554	1,225,458	506,480	778,672	598,050	1,625,391
RHODE ISLAND	42,613	106,529	42,346	64,966	45,116	118,967
SOUTH CAROLINA	213,714	509,059	161,448	182,250	184,347	380,643
SOUTH DAKOTA	81,841	90,703	25,008	36,329	46,212	96,541
TENNESSEE	332,520	860,276	252,479	286,075	301,124	597,962
TEXAS	1,832,872	2,534,915	739,138	835,764	974,204	1,870,059
UTAH	190,498	228,036	53,380	68,980	114,851	204,036
VERMONT	67,157	72,471	16,063	20,674	24,913	59,861
VIRGINIA	330,889	638,347	184,896	230,005	242,420	572,102
WASHINGTON	275,706	502,751	157,146	229,037	181,675	515,122
WEST VIRGINIA	80,775	269,492	93,579	109,600	101,413	261,989
WISCONSIN	413,805	803,692	254,670	363,547	340,512	732,124
WYOMING	46,664	46,765	12,311	19,471	21,881	57,715
TOTALS	17,747,849	36,061,610	11,142,994	13,932,549	13,503,611	28,311,931

*Telephone Numbers Available

5,000 minimum

121

To give you an example of the breadth of information available, the lists on the previous pages are examples you can purchase from Best Mailing Lists in New York City.

Association Memberships

Association memberships are another potential source of names for you for your surveys and later marketing efforts. More than 30,000 national and international organizations are in existence. They include:

Trade
Business and Commercial
Agricultural and Commodity
Legal, Governments, Public Administration, and Military
Scientific, Engineering, and Technical
Educational
Cultural
Social Welfare
Health and Medical
Public Affairs
Fraternal
Foreign Interest, Nationality, and Ethnic
Religious
Veterans, Hereditary, and Patriotic
Hobby and Vocational
Athletic and Sports
Labor Unions
Chambers of Commerce
Trade and Tourism
Greek Letter and Related Organizations
Fan Clubs

The *Encyclopedia of Associations,* which can be found in most libraries, lists all 30,000 complete with descriptions of the purpose of the associa-

Example: Encyclopedia of Associations Entry

★3276★ NATIONAL ASSOCIATION OF CONVENIENCE STORES (Retailing) (NACS)
1605 King St.   Phone: (703) 684-3600
Alexandria, VA 22314   Kerley LeBoeuf, Pres.
Founded: 1961. Members: 2300. Staff: 24. Budget: $6,100,000. Retail stores that sell gasoline, fast foods, soft drinks, dairy products, beer, cigarettes, publications, grocery items, snacks, and nonfood items and are usually open seven days per week for longer hours than conventional supermarkets. (Convenience stores generally stock 1500 to 3000 items, compared to 7000 or more in most supermarkets. NACS estimates there are some 69,200 convenience stores, most are chain owned, with 2000 more established each year in the suburbs and concentrated city areas.) Conducts educational, legislative, and fraternal activities; sponsors management seminars. Maintains information center, which includes 40 training films. Also maintains task forces; compiles statistics. **Computerized Services:** Convenience store industry and membership data base; mailing list. **Telecommunications Services:** Fax, (703)836-4564. **Committees:** Education/Research; Government Relations Specialists; Loss Control; Political Action.

Publications: *Compensation Survey*, annual. ● *FACT Book*, annual. ● *NACS SCAN*, monthly. Association and industry newsletter; includes book reviews. **Price:** Free. **Circulation:** 6000. **Advertising:** not accepted. ● *National Association of Convenience Stores—Membership and Services Directory*, annual. **Price:** Available to members only. **Circulation:** 4000. **Advertising:** not accepted. ● *National Association of Convenience Stores—State of the Industry Report*, annual. ● *Shop Talk Paper*, quarterly. ● *Washington Report*, biweekly. ● Also publishes manuals and issues training audiotapes.

Convention/Meeting: annual (with exhibits) - 1990 Sept. 23-26, Dallas, TX; 1991 Nov. 3-6, Orlando, FL; 1992 Oct. 25-28, Atlanta, GA; 1993 Sept. 19-22, San Francisco, CA; 1994 Oct. 16-19, New Orleans, LA.

tion, when it was founded, how many members it has, its publications, when it holds conventions, and much more:

The following key word list gives you an idea of the broad range of associations that list in the encyclopedia:

Academic Placement
AIDS
Alternative Medicine
Armed Forces
Bilingualism
Bronchoesophagology
Cerebral Palsy
Classical Studies
Cossack
Disc Sports
Elvis Presley
Experiential Education
Fluoridation
Gravitational Strain
Hoo Hoo
Intellectual Property
Labor
Lupus Erythematosus
Meat
Meeting Planners
Naturopathy
Packaging
Psychiatry
Pyrotechnics
Robotics
Sand Castles
Soil
Swiss
Tibetan
Tuna
Vegetarianism
Urine
Yoga
Zoroastrian

Accounting
Aikido
Appalachian
Awards
Book Clubs
Bulgaria
Circus
Contests
Crystallography
Disposable Products
Epilepsy
Finnish
Gospel
Handball
Impotence
Japan
Law
Marbles
Medical Examiners
Missing Persons
Occupational Medicine
Pituitary
Publishing
Rescue
Roller Coasters
Scientific Products
Speech
Telecommunications
Toxicology
Ultimatism
Violence
Witchcraft
Zoology

Directories

If you aren't totally exhausted from ordering mailing lists and contacting associations, or if you have not yet located clusters of potential customers, you may want to browse through *Directories in Print* to see if there are any specialized directories that can help. Formerly, the *Directory of Directories*, *Directories in Print* is an annotated guide of approximately 10,000 business and industrial directories, professional and scientific rosters, directory databases, and other lists and guides of all kinds that are published in the United States or that are national or regional in scope of interest. The categories included are:

General business
Specific industries and lines of business
Banking, finance, insurance, and real estate
Agriculture, resource industries, and the environment
Law, military, and the government
Science, engineering, and computer science
Education
Information science, social science, and linguistics
Biography
Arts and entertainment
Public affairs and social concerns
Health and medicine
Religious, ethnic, and fraternal affairs
Genealogical, veterans, and patriotic affairs
Hobbies, travel, and leisure
Sports and outdoor recreation

On the next page is a typical entry.

Obtaining Valid Customer Feedback

Once you have obtained lists of potential customers, those people can be surveyed using whatever method suits you best. The main point to remember is that people need to be selected randomly (which means that everyone on a list has an equal chance of being selected as a respondent)

Example: Directories in Print Entry

★2766★ **Directory of Home Furnishings Retailers**
Chain Store Guide Information Services
425 Park Ave.
New York, NY 10022   Phone: (212)371-9400
Covers: Nearly 5,300 furniture retailers that operate approximately 13,510 stores; nearly 60 wholesale furniture distributors. **Entries include:** Company name, address, phone, fax, products, key personnel, year established, sales range, number of stores, total square feet, rating of price range, furniture styles, stock purchases from distributors; decorator services, furniture rentals, and contract furniture are offered. **Arrangement:** Geographical. **Indexes:** Company name. **Pages (approx.):** 1,600. **Frequency:** Annual, August. **Editor(s):** Kevin Edison. **Price:** $259.00, plus $5.00 shipping. **Fax:** (212)826-6390. **Other formats:** Mailing labels.

so that your results won't be biased. I usually do my choosing of participants the old-fashioned way—by closing my eyes and touching spots on the list and then listing all the names I've touched until I reach the number I need. If you are uncomfortable with this primitive method, there are many more sophisticated methods, and some mailing companies may be willing to send you lists which have already been selected randomly. A good research firm or university professor can help.

Finally, keep surveying people until you get at least a twenty to thirty percent response rate to your interview. I actually go for at least 40 percent or 50 percent because the information is so critical. Because this level of response can take a great deal of effort (and no small amount of nagging), many of my clients are satisfied with lower response rates. Again, it's your decision. Just remember that the more information you can gather before you roll out a new product line or whenever you need customer feedback, the better off you'll be.

The Competition

The Moment of Truth

Next to knowing what your customers want, the most important thing is knowing who your competitors are and what they are doing. Many companies try to skip this ninth step, only to learn later that it cost them time, money and customers. Every product has competition. Many years ago I heard of a company in the Midwest that developed a fail-safe laser beam protective system for warehouses. It was to be the first one on the market. The company believed that it had no competition. Indeed, technically, it didn't. There weren't any other laser beam protective systems in the marketplace at that time. What they discovered was that not only did they have competition, but that their competition was fierce. It was inexpensive, easily replaceable, dependable, was easy to care for, and had customer loyalty—it was dogs! I don't know if that company's product ever did make it to market.

Assume you have competition, even if you are developing a new industry. Your first task regarding your competition is to describe where it will come from in generic terms. For example, accounting firms that provide consulting services for start-up companies in Michigan are competition for my strategic planning and market work for companies in the Midwest. Business school professors who consult are competition; their students are competition; other consultants are competition, even free services offered by small business centers are competition for me.

Exercise 9-1

Take time to describe your competition generally. Don't stop at one type of company or product, because competition almost always comes from more than one direction.

_____

_____

_____

_____

_____

_____

Exercise 9-2

When you are done with your general list, list names, addresses, phone numbers, and the contact person for each competitor.

Competitor One:

Address:

Phone:

Contact Person:

Competitor Two:

Address:

Phone:

Contact Person:

Competitor Three:

Address:

Phone:

Contact Person:

If you haven't identified at least three competitive firms or types of competitors, you need to keep thinking. On the other hand, if you've named more than a dozen competitors, you are probably either worrying too much or have identified a market that is too big to go after in any rational way. In either case, you want to rethink both your market and who represents the competition in that market.

Now is also the time to start a file on the companies you have discovered. This should be updated continuously. A good way to keep track of competition is to get yourself on competitors' mailing lists, particularly for press releases regarding new products. It is also worth regularly reviewing your industry's trade press (in case your competitors refuse to put you on any mailing lists!). You also can subscribe to the local newspapers where your competition is headquartered so that you can read their help

THE COMPETITION

Date   Initials   Source

Company

Address   Telephone

Company Strengths   Company Weaknesses

Product

Product Strengths   Product Weaknesses

Market Share

Sales

Net Income

New Products

Comments

Date   Initials   Source

Company

Address   Telephone

Company Strengths   Company Weaknesses

Product

Product Strengths   Product Weaknesses

Market Share

Sales

Net Income

New Products

Comments

THE COMPETITION

Date   Initials   Source

Company

Address   Telephone

Company Strengths	Company Weaknesses

Product

Product Strengths	Product Weaknesses

Market Share

Sales

Net Income

New Products

Comments

wanted ads, new product summaries, management appointments, and chief executive officer speeches.

Exercise 9-3

The following form will help to organize the information you find. No matter what industry you are in, you will have at least three competitors, so we have included three forms in the workbook to get you started.

Exercise 9-4

If you are in a large market, filling out a market matrix might help you to sort through your competition. A matrix is like a checkerboard that has specific qualities represented by each square on the board. One square could be cheap with no service, another could be expensive with a service warranty included in the price. A picture best communicates what I am describing.

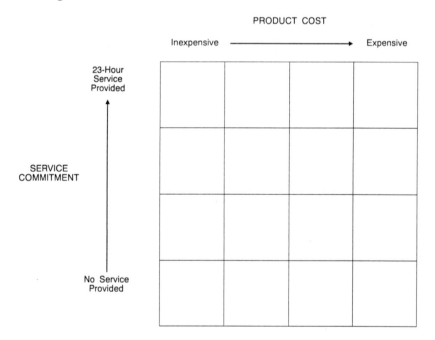

Now, for each product that is possible competition, write the name of its parent company in the box that best defines where the product stands in your marketplace. If you do not know the product and companies by now, go back to all the sources you used to do your environmental analysis in the first few chapters; try to get enough data to put each product somewhere in the box.

After you have written everyone else's product name in your matrix, write in yours. The companies that are closest to you will be your toughest competition.

Exercise 9-5: Competition Strengths and Weaknesses

It is useful to list the specific names of your competitors as well as their strengths and weaknesses on a page if possible so that you can regularly refer back to it. Remember that the strengths and weaknesses you are interested in are *relative to your customers,* not you. As an example, you may think that the bank that competes with you hires people who have no idea how to manage their time because every time you go in there everyone is chatting. Your customers may have a very different opinion. They may perceive that bank as being very friendly and as giving terrific customer service. On the chart then, their chattiness is a strength, not a weakness. Write your analysis here:

Competitor	Strengths	Weaknesses

Neutralizing Competition Strengths

After you spend time going over the strengths you have listed, it is important to think through actions that could either turn their strengths into weaknesses or to compete with their strengths in other ways. Don't be discouraged if you can't respond to each strength—not even Xerox has all of its market. On the other hand, if you can't do anything about any of the strengths you have listed, you may want to reconsider your product.

One more point before you complete the next exercise. Unless your market is very price sensitive (and you'll know whether it is by now) try not to make the price of your product less than your competition as a way of competing with their product. It doesn't serve any real purpose and could put you out of business. I remember a computer software company that cut the price of its software to several dollars less than its competition. Unfortunately, the company lost a dollar every time it sold a piece of software as a result, leading to bankruptcy.

Exercise 9-6

What can you do to neutralize your competitors' strengths:

COMPETITOR STRENGTH	NEUTRALIZING ACTION

_____

_____

_____

_____

_____

_____

_____

_____

If there is one universal truth about competition, it is that surprises will come from somewhere you never considered. A fun exercise is to invite a group of friends over if you are a single entrepreneur, or to have a group meeting if you have any colleagues in your business, to brainstorm where surprises could lurk. Remember to use the correct ground rules for brainstorming (i.e., set a time limit; make yourselves think quickly; don't criticize anything someone else says; list all ideas). Once you have brainstormed ideas, brainstorm responses that could control the impact of competition on your efforts.

Exercise 9-7

List both the surprises and how you could respond:

SURPRISES	RESPONSES

Exercise 9-8

Now flip your thinking around a little. Pretend your competition is analyzing you and your product at the same time. What will they try to do when you introduce your product to the market? How will you respond?

_____

_____

_____

_____

_____

_____

The Art of Finding Out About Competition

What if you haven't been able to fill out all the forms in this chapter so far? You won't be alone. Unlike corporations such as AT&T, most of us can't afford to put together sophisticated electronic intelligence networks to track our competition. In fact, the person usually responsible for finding out what the competition is doing is the person who decides that getting the information is important. Invariably, that person also has at least one full-time job already. On the other hand, not paying attention to the activities of the other people in your industry can destroy a company, and quickly. Remember that, in the end, what every company should be looking for is a competitive advantage in their market.

What's a competitive advantage? It's a new process or product feature change (or these days, even a packaging change) that makes your customers come to you first for a solution to their problem. By tracking your competition, you'll be able to know constantly what the competitive advantage of your product must be. In addition, keeping an eye on your competition will help you to:

✦ avoid surprises;

✦ be able to separate rumor from reality;

✦ identify threats to your market position; and

✦ identify new opportunities in the marketplace.

Unfortunately, not all information is created equally, nor is information equally easy to access. In his excellent book, *Competitive Analysis*, Leonard Fuld shares some "intelligence factors" that will tell you, even before you start to analyze your competition, how easy or difficult information will be to find—regardless of the type of information you need. First of all, if you are a local or regional firm competing with other local or regional companies, it will be much easier to locate information than in situations where your competition and its operating territories are both national. The more dynamic and actively growing your industry is, the easier it should be to get information. For example, it is fairly easy to locate information related to telecommunications but difficult to find out how privately held retail chains are faring. That's the good news. The bad news is that much of the information is inaccurate in "hot" industries because rumors are rampant. The more regulated an industry is, the easier it is to obtain data because government agencies hold information, and many agencies are required by law to share what they have through various types of freedom of information acts. Two good examples are the medical industry and the hazardous waste industry.

Given these factors, how do you actually go about getting competitive information? First, you need to know the types of information you seek. It turns out that four types of information sources exist: basic written, basic verbal, creative written and creative verbal. You already know that your goal is to zero in on sources that will supply you with both timely and highly specific information about a company.

Well, it turns out that you may need a combination of all four of these types of information to get data that is truly useful to you. Basic sources of information come from the "horse's mouth." These are sources of information that you get directly from a company. One example is an annual report. Another might be a company press release. I always try to get on my competition's mailing list so that I can get their press releases of new product announcements. It's amazing how generous companies can be with their information. Or, you can go to listen to a speech by a company's president.

I can remember some great IBM stories from my childhood on this. The way I remember them, Tom Watson, Jr., who was president, used to get really excited whenever there was some new product breakthrough in the labs. Like most company presidents, he liked sharing the good news; it kept IBM at the forefront of the computer industry. The only problem was that his sharing could be premature, which meant that any of his competitors who may be in the audience (and they were there!) were getting terrific information "from the horse's mouth."

Unfortunately, these basic sources of information may not be readily available to you. There are times when some of us can't afford to fly to California or Wichita or Tampa whenever our competitor's president is speaking. And written information is not available from many, if not most, privately held companies. In these situation, you have to be creative.

Creative sources of information are surrogate sources. For example, say you can't get a hold of your competition's income statement. What could help you piece one together? Well, counting the average number of cars in the employee's parking lot over the course of the month would probably give you a fairly good idea of the number of employees. State and local economic development staff will be able to give you labor rates. Local realtors will know the value of the property and whether the company leases or owns the land. Box suppliers can tell you about plant production. Alumni records from your local university might be able to provide information about key staff. The company's help wanted ads can give you clues about job responsibilities of key staff, so you can estimate salaries. Each of these is an example of a creative source of information.

As you may already have noticed, information can either be written or verbal. Regarding competitive analysis, my preference always has been verbal information because it tends to be more current than written information. For example, most annual reports are at least a few months old by the time they are published. From the perspective of competitive analysis, this written information is not particularly timely. I try to collect all four types of information about competitors: basic written, basic verbal, creative written, and creative verbal. I've learned that depending on one source can be dangerous because the company could be deliberately misleading or overly optimistic through annual reports or product releases. Or, rumors could have taken the place of real information, as is true for much trade show gossip. You want to use all four and gather information until the sources start to tell you the same thing about the company. The chart at the top of the next page outlines the types of sources you need.

The process of gathering information is fairly straightforward once you know to track down both verbal and written sources from the company (if you can) and from outside sources.

When I start to gather information, I first take time to develop an information-gathering strategy. In other words, I develop a priority list of the sources that I want to tap, starting with what I think the best sources will

	WRITTEN	VERBAL
BASIC	Example: A company's annual report	Example: A speech by the president of the company
CREATIVE	Example: State records regarding loans to the company	Example: Local real estate agents

be and working my way down to sources I believe will provide only marginal information. Then, I work through the list, making sure to use all of the types of information, until I feel like information is being repeated often. At that point, I normally have a fairly accurate picture of the activities of my competitors. One under-used source of information is made up of articles in newspapers and industry journals. The trick is to milk them by pretending that you are looking for clues in a good mystery. People mentioned in the article may be worth interviewing; the writer may be a source of information. If there is a bibliography, it can lead you to additional sources of information.

I find that I use several key sources repeatedly to gather competitive information:

Associations: Assume your industry has an association until you know better. Call yours. Associations provide reports, journals, industry analyses, as well as organize trade shows and other types of events. Trade association staff for the larger associations can be very helpful, particularly those responsible for the associations written materials. If the executive director is very active and spends his or her time at trade shows and seminars, then he/she also could be helpful.

Local business newspapers: In Detroit and Chicago, for example, *Crain's* is a wonderful source of information about privately held companies.

Business reporters: They know a lot about everyone. Information gathering and sharing is their business. I have found that business reporters are most willing to talk to me if I first give them information that is useful to them.

The Yellow Pages: They list all of the competitors in a geographical area, suppliers and even product lines in cases where the competition chooses to advertise.

Trade magazines: Whether or not these are published by associations, trade magazines are also wonderful sources of information. Their personnel announcements will help you to spot major management changes. Help wanted ads provide information, as do new product announcements, events calendars, advance trade show information, and special surveys.

People: People who work directly in the area you are investigating can be very helpful. For instance, if you are trying to find the volume shipped by your competitor, you might want to first go to your own company's shipping department and ask staff members what they would do to find out the volume. The trick here is to ask yourself who the person is "in the know"; the person who can either give you or lead you to the answers you really need.

There is a broad variety of verbal sources available to you. Another source available to everyone is a good librarian. (I know you would have guessed this by now.) I am always impressed with the breadth of knowledge and proficiency of the librarians in my community. Remember, they are helping their clients to find all types of information every day. The best seem to be business school librarians, because their focus is on researching corporate and related sources of information.

Industry experts are obvious verbal sources. They can be found by reading articles about the industry, by attending trade shows, and by going to seminars on topics relevant to your business. You may have to buy their time, but, if you've found the right person, it will be worth it. Often they already have done all the research you are about to undertake. At a minimum, they should have useful suggestions regarding possible written sources of information for you.

In the same vein, university professors can be useful, if you can get their attention. Like industry experts, professors often already have done the research you are planning. In my experience, the most helpful academics have been:

+ business school professors in marketing, finance, and sometimes organizational development;

+ public policy related academics; and

+ labor relations academics.

I also have learned that the caliber or size of the school is not necessarily an indicator of how useful their information will be to you. Professors from small, local universities and colleges usually have been very accessible and willing to help me on research projects. Even better, occasionally one of my clients has ended up as a graduate student "project," meaning that someone else is collecting useful information for the company—at no cost to the company.

Finally, it is worth your time to find marketing professionals with experience in your industry. They are in the business of discovering, analyzing, and making use of information in a way that serves marketing purposes. Don't be afraid to hire outside marketing consultants when you need them. A good consultant can extend your own capabilities by providing expertise that you may not have. He or she can give you a fresh perspective by serving as an objective sounding board. You may find that, even though you think you have collected legitimate information from your customers over time, a good consultant often can get better or more in-depth information as an outsider.

How do you find consultants if you decide to use one? The American Marketing Association (AMA) Directory. For information, you can call the association in Chicago at (312) 648-0536. Your local telephone yellow pages list marketing consultants, as do most Chamber of Commerce directories. The main thing to remember is that you never want to hire some-one without:

+ interviewing the person first;

+ seeing samples of their work;

+ asking for references; and

+ calling the references.

A recent source of help is made up of former librarians who have started their own information research services in which they search through written sources of information via databases for you. Most can access libraries, universities, laboratories, and information clearinghouses all over the world. And most are very reasonably priced.

There are also many public written sources of information available to you. I use two types. One is public filings, (federal, state, and local). At the national level, the Security and Exchange Commission requires dozens of reports from public companies, such as 10-K reports, which are annual financial reports; 10-Q reports, which are quarterly financial filings; and proxies, which are special event reports given to stockholders. You could order information by mail from the Commission, but that can be too slow. Call Disclosure, Inc. at 800-638-8241. It's a private company in Washington that is the Commission's sole vender for the private reproduction and distribution of report findings. Reports are inexpensive, usually under $20.

The second public source of information is called "Current Industrial Reports" and is published by the U.S. Department of Commerce. It has timely data on production, inventories, and orders for 5,000 products (40 percent of U.S. manufacturing). It can help you define market attributes, the strongest selling products for an industry, shipment patterns, etc. The reports cover all major industries: food, textile, apparel, wood, paper, chemicals, rubber, clay, primary metals, intermediate metals, electrical, etc. To get current industrial reports you can write to Customer Services, Bureau of Census, Washington D.C. 20233, or find a good business library.

There is a down side to public information. It isn't timely, and it doesn't give management information, changes in organizational structure, mar-keting plans, or new product introductions. Don't depend too heavily on public sources.

D atabases

A database is a collection or pool of information that is recorded, indexed, and stored in a computer. The positives: thousands of pieces of information; the negatives: much of the information can be obsolete. The best databases are actually groupings of hundreds of other databases.

BRS

BRS requires a monthly subscription fee. For that fee, however, it offers immediate discounts on all the databases in its system. Also, its search language is pretty easy to understand.

DIALOG

Dialog offers the largest selection of databases, with more than 200. It covers a broad assortment of technical and general interest fields. It is clear and well organized.

NEXIS

(Also LEXIS for Law) Nexis contains entire articles, not just abstracts, and large newspaper selections, including the *New York Times.*

SDC/ORBIT

This system is best known for its scientific and technical data use, offering more than 80 databases.

There are many other databases available. Most database vendors, including these four, can act as an automated monitoring service for you, sending you the latest information on your competition and industry. This service is called Selective Discrimination of Information (SDI), and is inexpensive and ongoing.

For marketing research software, you can contact the American Marketing Association in Chicago at (312) 648-0536. The association compiles an annual directory of marketing research software that can be very helpful. Many of the Big Six accounting firms offer this service to their clients as well.

Example: Databases Available for Market Research

Business: PTS Promt, ABI/Inform, *The Wall Street Journal*, Trade & Industry Index, Harvard Business Review.

Technology: Compendex, Computer Database, World Patent Abstracts, Computer Intelligence.

Demographics: Donnelley Demographics, Cendata.

Law and Government: Commerce Business Daily, LEXIS, Laborlaw, Federal Register.

Energy and Environment: Hazardous Waste News, Energyline, Environmental Bibliography, Pollution Abstracts.

Health Care: Pharmaceutical News Index, Health Planning and Administration, Medicine.

Company Financials: Compact Disclosure, Media General, D&B Credit Reports.

International: Nikkei Telecom, Xinhua English Language News, Key British Enterprises, Kyodo News Service, Canadian Dun's Market Identifiers.

News Wires: Dow Jones News, AP, UPI, Jiji Press Ticker Service, Businesswire.

Industry Reports

Industry reports are a primary information source. I almost always start here when I am researching a new industry. There is a surprisingly broad range of industry reports available. For example, Dun and Bradstreet writes industry reports on an ongoing basis. So does Standard and Poor's. As I mentioned earlier, most journals publish forecast issues, which look ahead and backwards for specific industries. General business magazines such as *Fortune, Forbes,* and *Business Week* also include major industry analyses fairly regularly.

Another source of industry information comes from brokerage houses such as Merrill Lynch and Paine Webber. As a small but loyal Merrill Lynch client, I have come to look forward to a quality look at key industries and other economic trends that I receive care of my broker. Universities often assign industry report tasks to students who obviously are motivated to do a thorough and timely job. These are worth checking out, as are individual industry surveys done by independent market research firms. As always, a competent librarian can be very helpful.

If you are wondering where to start, a good place is the U.S. Department of Commerce annual *U.S. Industrial Outlook*. This tome reviews over 300 industries and is published every January. Its biggest emphasis seems to be manufacturing. Although the actual discussion of each industry is short, I've been impressed with Commerce's assessment of the particular industry prospects over the next three to five years. The *Outlook* also contains a great deal of statistical information, summarized from census data, which saves you the time you might otherwise spend wading through the census information. Finally, authors usually list sources of information for readers hungry for more data— again saving you time.

Standard and Poor's Industry Surveys are my second favorite source of industry information. These also are done annually; quarterly updates are available. If you are interested in a non-manufacturing industry, you might want to start with these surveys; half of the reports cover service and retail industries. Standard and Poor's staff focus less on describing the industry and more on outlook. If you use these surveys, be sure not to forget to look for both the annual analysis and the current analysis.

Other sources of industry reports include:

National Association of Manufacturers (202) 637-3000

Predicast Forecasts (216) 795-3000: A quarterly report for industries that features short- and long-range forecasts as well as the industry's predicted growth rate.

Industry Forecast (914) 238-3665: Published 12 times per year.

Industrial Statistics Yearbook 1-800-553-3210: General industry statistics.

The Structure of U.S. Business (212) 697-6080: This is an analysis of employment trends in industry.

Trade Associations

Trade associations were introduced earlier. In addition to associations related to your own industry, there are several marketing associations that you can tap for suggestions regarding books, journals, and experts in your geographical area. Marketing associations exist for most industry groups. To find them, you can skim the Encyclopedia of Associations. To my knowledge, the American Marketing Association (AMA) in Chicago is the largest association that exists which is focused solely on marketing. With more than 53,000 members, the organization defines itself as a "professional society of marketing and marketing research executives, sales and promotion managers, advertising specialists, teachers, and others interested in marketing." The organization promotes research related to marketing, and sponsors seminars and more than thirty annual conferences. (Should you decide that marketing is your future, the AMA also offers a placement service). Its library has more than 5,000 volumes. The following publications are also put together by the AMA:

American Marketing Association—Proceedings

The Annual Marketing Services Guide

The International Membership Directory

Journal of Health Care Marketing

Journal of Marketing

Journal of Marketing Research

Marketing News

Marketing Research

To contact the American Marketing Association, you can write to 250 S. Wacker Drive, Suite 200, Chicago, IL 60606 or call (312) 648-0536. Other associations that may be helpful include:

American Mail-Order Association: 444 Lincoln Blvd., #107, Venice, CA 90291.

American Telemarketing Association: (818) 995-7338

Direct Marketing Association: (212) 768-7277

Marketing Research Association: (312) 644-6610

National Account Marketing Association: (212) 983-5140

National Mail Order Association: (213) 934-7986

Society for Marketing Professional Services: (703) 549-6117

Women in Advertising and Marketing: (301) 369-7400

Once you gather all your information, how should you put it all together? Sources of information are described in greater length in Leonard Fuld's book, *Monitoring the Competition*. I've given an example of a competitive analysis below:

Example: Competitive Analysis

Sweet Baby Boy, Inc.

Company Background: Sweet Baby Boy, Inc. was started to design and manufacture gender neutral clothes for baby boys up to the age of two years. The outfits include sweatshirts, overalls, and one-piece jumpsuits. Each outfit has a theme such as a cuddly bear, or precious pony that is reflected in hand-painted designs on the outfit. Sweet Baby Boy, Inc. has targeted its products to higher income households with significant discretionary income (i.e., to families who can afford to spend up to $100 on an outfit for a baby boy).

Analysis: Four companies compete with Sweet Baby Boy, Inc. for the young children's upscale play clothes market.

Competitor	Strengths	Weaknesses	Neutralizer
Sweethearts	Well defined image, cute look, strong staff	Too narrow focus, too expensive	Lighter, quality fabrics, no country designs, less expensive
Omygoodness	Large product line, cute design, well known, durable excellent distribution well matched clothes	Too common, "macho"	Unique designs
Cuddly, Inc.	Product made off-shore, unusual designs	No toddler, not widely distributed	Toddler line increasing distribution, building loyalty
Little Bear	Widely distributed, less costly	Sloppy look not unique	Cute, unique designs

Through its choice of fabrics, designs, and cost controls, Sweet Baby Boy, Inc. has developed a strong competitive position in this market. That position can best be described by the following attributes of each of our products:

+ gender neutral;

+ unique styling, not faddish;

+ identifiable by design;

+ very attractive styles, use of light-colored fabrics, and special trims;

+ elegant and clean play wear;

+ practical fabrics; and

+ competitive prices.

In summary, Sweet Baby Boy, Inc.'s market position is that it designs, manufacturers, and sells unique, gender neutral, competitively priced play wear made of practical fabric for little boys.

Exercise 9-9

Take time here to summarize your analysis of your competition. Using the material you have written in the competition charts, write several paragraphs describing where your competition will come from, and what you can do about it. If you can, end your discussion with a summary of the strengths you think you can depend on, even with competition, to give your company the sales that you want.

COMPETITIVE ANALYSIS:

_____

_____

_____

_____

_____

_____

_____

_____

_____

Positioning

How Market Positions Work

In its own way, your tenth step summarizes everything you've done to now. All your thinking about your product—the environmental analysis, figuring out what your market is, what its trends are, and who your competitors are—is really geared toward one goal. That goal is figuring out what your position is in your market. Here's an oversimplified example of positioning; it will make long-term marketing professionals cringe, but it still gives you a first taste of the positioning concept.

I grew up in a family with four girls who were very close in age, about a year and a half apart. Worse, we all looked a lot alike. As a result, to make ourselves uniquely recognizable both to our harried parents and the outside world, we each developed unique identities. One of us became the ballerina, one went for the pretty sister, one was the jock; I held out for "smart sister." As a result, people were able to separate us from the crowd by describing the pertinent sister as "she's the jock," or "she's the smart one." What they were describing was our position in the family.

Now, for a more formal definition of positioning: "The positioning concept begins with the idea that customers choose products based on the benefits they expect the product to deliver. For example, a product such as a personal computer may be expected to provide speed, accuracy, low cost, reliability, compatibility with a wide range of software, availability of service when needed, and so forth. A laundry detergent such as Tide may provide good cleaning ability, whitening agents, stain removal and the like." (From *How to Write a Marketing Plan*, by Herbert Hennessey and Robert Kopp, American Management Association, p. 6.)

You actually have three "positions:"

1. The product position, which is how your product is perceived by your market.

2. Your market position, which is the actual response of your customers to your product.

3. Your company's position, which is the reputation of your company in your market.

Of these, the product position is the most critical piece right now. Once you actually start selling your product, then the actual market position, and your company position, will become increasingly important. Before you try a detailed description of your product position, go back to the matrix you drew in Chapter Nine. What was your product's position there? In other words, what benefits will your customers expect from your product?

Before you answer, let me share some words of wisdom:

Don't forget to include intangible factors in your description of your position. One of the ironies of marketing new products is how important intangible attributes are in the selling of a product. For example, how many people tried Bartles and Jaymes wine coolers just because the television commercials made the product sound like fun?

Try to focus on your defined target market at first. Otherwise you could have so much information to sift through that it could all become useless. A quick test of whether you are in over your head is to ask yourself periodically if you are trying to make the product be too many things to too many people. If you are, you need to narrow your focus, quickly.

Also, be prepared to shift your position quickly if your environment (remember the environmental analysis you did?) changes.

Positioning criteria

Normally, a market position can be defined by considering seven product attributes:

1. The price of the product and the importance of price in the eyes of the consumer.

2. Service, i.e., how much service is provided along with the product.

3. Technology, i.e., whether or not the technology related to the product is important to the customer.

4. The product's application, i.e., whether it can serve many different purposes or has only one purpose. For example, most medical devices only have one purpose. In contrast, monogrammed leather has many purposes. It can be used for furniture, cars, briefcases, clothes, shoes, etc. As a result, it is a product with a broad application.

5. Quality, i.e., how important quality is to your customers. I can tell you that quality is one of the most important product attributes of the 1990s.

6. Distribution channels, i.e., all the methods you will use to get your product into the hands of your customers.

7. Market tastes. This is a catch-all attribute that gives you an opportunity to think about other things that matter specifically to the target market you have identified.

With these comments in mind, you need to describe your product's position in detail. Some position statements are listed below to give you examples.

Example: Market Attributes

PRICE
Our product will be the least expensive toothbrush on the market.

SERVICE
As an innovation for this market, a year-long warranty will be included in the price of the toothbrush.

Or
Customers may call 1-800-TOO-MUCH twenty-four hours a day if they need assistance with their product.

TECHNOLOGY
XYZ's microwave is the most advanced of its kind.

PRODUCT APPLICATION
The toothbrush has several uses, including doubling as a scrub brush.

QUALITY
Our engine is made of the strongest composite plastic available today.

DISTRIBUTION CHANNELS
Our paperclips will be sold through a direct sales force; each sales representative will be responsible for a three-state region.

MARKET TASTES

All of our product surfaces are sanded to a shiny smoothness and painted in pastel colors, reflecting the current tastes of the teen-age market.

You may discover that you do not need to consider categories of attributes for your product. As an example, people who buy Mercedes generally still buy a Mercedes, regardless of price. Several thousand dollar variations in price do not seem to matter too much. As a result, price is not one of the key attributes of a Mercedes. On the other hand, quality and value might be.

Now, choosing the attributes that matter the most to your target market, summarize the attributes of your product in paragraph form. Start with a summary sentence that tells what your position will be in your market. For example, "Faxall will be the Xerox of the fax machine industry." Then use your positioning sentences as "proof" for your statement. Your reader should end up with a very clear picture of where your product would fall in any market, comparing your product with competitive ones. Normally, customers care most about two or three attributes so you might want to focus on them.

Example: Market Position

Jamie B's All Natural Bird Feeders

The market for bird feeders is close to a $20 million market in the U.S. alone. Jamie B's bird feeder is made of a large pine cone, only found in British Columbia. The cone is dipped into fast drying honey and then into birdseed. It is finished with a big fat pine green ribbon.

Market Position: The market position for Jamie B's All Natural Bird Feeders is that they are all natural, inexpensive, attractive bird feeders. Prices for bird feeders on the market run from $5 to $50 or more. Most sell for less than $20. Jamie B's will be the least expensive bird feeder on the market at $3.97.

No specific customer services will be provided although an "800" telephone number will be listed on the packaging for questions and comments. The quality of the product will be top-notch. No broken cones will be sold. The bird feeders will be distributed through two channels. First, the company has a contract with K Mart and Sears to sell the products. Second, the feeder will be sold through sales representatives, and at local garden and feed stores. To date, orders have been received with 3,000 other stores in the Midwest.

Finally, and most importantly, the feeder is environmentally safe and mixes in well with natural settings. This is, perhaps, the most important product attribute. No other bird feeder on the market is all natural. The cone's inherent loveliness is appealing to customers looking for products complimentary to the environment.

Your positioning, if you have only one product, will reflect your company's market position. If you are developing multiple products, then together they may change your market position slightly. At the same time, your product position also will be the first factor defining your company's position in your market.

Product Requirements

Product requirements evolve out of all the marketing research and thinking you've done so far. By the time you know who your customers are, your competition and market position, you should have a very clear idea of what your product needs to do, look like, its price, and how you should deliver it to your customers. Taken together, a product's functions, appearance, price, packaging, and delivery are summarized in a market plan as product requirements.

Tangible Features

The physical features of the product are features that you can define through your senses. Included are the appearance of the product, its size, it's composition, color, smell, and shape.

Intangible Features

These features are subjective evaluations of the use of a product. Intangible features reflect the benefits that your customers think they will get. For example, Rolex watches are perceived as signifying wealth of a certain kind, and of being stylish.

Defining the actual requirements of your product is an exercise in taking the needs, wants, and values that you have been describing for your market and translating them into physical features that will satisfy those needs more effectively and efficiently than any of your competitors. It is worth taking a couple of minutes to review everything that you have written in this book up to now as well as any notes you have made or survey results you have collected, before you answer the following questions:

Exercise 10-1

What problem is your product solving?

_____

_____

How will it need to function?

_____

_____

What size will it need to be?

_____

_____

What is its preferred color?

_____

_____

Should it have a smell? (Don't laugh. Smell is fast emerging as one of "the" product features of the 1990s. Have you ever noticed how the smell of fresh cookies at a shopping mall somehow results in your making a purchase you never planned?)

_____

_____

What are its technical specifications?

Should it be easy to handle?

Of what material does it need to be made?

Is instructional material needed?

Does it need to be simple to demonstrate?

Can it be repaired?

Product Feature Example

Whacko Greeting Cards

Background: Whacko Greeting Cards are targeted to professionals from the ages 25 to 50. The cards celebrate unusual milestones such as lay-offs, burnout, divorces, car trouble, etc.

Product Requirements: Whacko Greeting Cards need to be sized large enough to be mailed, but less than 8" by 11" in size. They should be brightly colored—preferably in bright greens, pinks, and yellows. Although pictures are unnecessary, the copy must be humorous in a *New Yorker* cartoon or Gary Larson style. Customers need to feel cheered up as a result of reading the cards. The cards should be available in locally-owned book and gift shops, preferably near a cafe or frozen yogurt shop.

Exercise 10-2

Describe your product's features here.

_____

_____

_____

_____

_____

_____

P ricing

Pricing can be as complicated as you want to make it. Most companies develop a price strategy by figuring out what their customers think a product is worth and then charging that price, regardless of the costs of production. This can be dangerous. If your customers think that you are making too big a profit, they won't buy the product. On the other hand, if your price doesn't at least cover your costs of production, you could sell yourself into bankruptcy. So what do you do? If you have no idea you might want to start out with prices that are the same as your competitors (as long as your production costs are covered) and see how they work out. As you get to know your market, you will gain a better sense of the price range that best matches your market's perceptions of the value of your product.

Some companies introduce new products with "penetration pricing." In penetration pricing, companies try to keep their product prices low when they first introduce the product to the market. The reason for the low price is to encourage potential customers to try the products. Food companies frequently do this. Then, price is raised gradually to cover costs and a reasonable profit.

Before you think about pricing any further, think about your industry for a couple of minutes. Is it price sensitive? Remember, the way to tell is to watch the behavior of your customers when they buy products similar to or competitive with yours. In other words, do people buy more of those products if the prices go down? Or less of the product if the prices go up? If the answer is yes, then demand for the product is elastic. And the customers in your market are price sensitive.

In some industries, the price does not have much of an impact. People who want to buy a Jaguar seem to still buy it even when the prices increase significantly, as they have in the past year, and I have mentioned Mercedes already. Here the demand for the product is not elastic. A point here: most people assume that their customers are more price sensitive than they really are. One of the biggest mistakes many of my clients make is assuming that their market is price sensitive without really watching the behavior of their customers. One of my favorite stories related to this is about a woman who owned a Native American jewelry store. When she left the shop for a couple of hours one day, she left a note for the assistant which said something like "change all prices 2/1." Well, the assistant wasn't sure what that meant, so he doubled the price of everything in the store. That afternoon, the store sold more items than ever before. It's a good thing the assistant didn't realize that the customers were supposed to get two pieces for the price of one!

In the 1990s what people care about is quality and the consistency of that quality. We may be willing to pay better than bottom line prices for that value, so don't short-change yourself.

If you know how elastic the demand for your product is in your market, your pricing decision should be straightforward. Keep your prices as low as possible in elastic markets; raise them when the demand is not elastic.

Another issue: Most companies give discounts to customers who either buy large quantities of their products or pay for their products when they get them. If you will be able to provide discount prices, you need to note that pricing in your actual market plan once you've put all these pieces together.

The following questions will help you to figure out what the best price for your product should be:

Exercise 10-3

What is the cost of production for each product?

What are the overhead expenses that need to be included in the price of each product? Remember that marketing costs need to come in here somewhere. You will be spending money on customer surveys, advertising, market research, brochures, etc., and that needs to be worked into your price as well.

What is the sum of the two? This is the minimum price you can charge for your product and still stay in business.

If you are sane, you will want to make some profit. What is the amount that you want to make on each product sale? If you are unsure, look at the averages for your industry. A good banker, accountant, or industry analyst can help you.

Add your profit to your first sum. That is your initial product price.

Before you write it down anywhere, you need to consider a couple more issues:

First of all, is your industry price sensitive?

If your answer is yes, what is the price of your closest competitor's product?

Can you sell your product for slightly less and still cover costs and make some profit?

Remembering that if your price is too low your customers will think that you are cutting quality, at what price can you sell your product?

In a price sensitive market, the price you just wrote down should be the price of your product.

If at any time in this exercise you come up with a price that will not cover your production costs and overhead, STOP. Do not produce the product; it will put you out of business as soon as you start selling it.

Go back to the question of price sensitivity. If the market is NOT price sensitive, would they pay MORE for a new product that can compete with what they are already buying, particularly if you are offering consistent good quality?

If your answer is yes, how do you know?

How much more would they pay?

Now add the additional amount to your original price. That is the price at which you should be able to sell your product in an inelastic market.

Are you willing to give discounts for large purchases?

If yes, how much of a discount? If you aren't sure about the amount, ask folks in your industry what the standard practice is.

Are you willing to give discounts for immediate payments?

If yes, how much of a discount? Again, if you aren't sure about amounts ask other folks in your industry.

Check yourself again to make certain that, even without discounts, you can cover all your costs with prices you've decided to use.

Exercise 10-4

By now you should have a fairly good idea of what your pricing practices will be. Before you commit to it, test it out. Call a couple of potential customers. Tell them your pricing strategy, including your discount policy.

What are their reactions?

_____

_____

_____

Taken together, their feedback will tell you whether or not the market is willing to pay the price you want to charge, and if not, what price they would pay.

Given the feedback, what is your product price?

_____

_____

_____

What is your discount policy?

_____

_____

_____

Distribution

Distribution is your strategy for getting your product into your customers' hands. How you choose to distribute the product is an important marketing question. Two basic methods of distribution exist: direct sales and indirect sales. If you can sell your product directly, I say do it. The reason is that it will help you to stay closer to your customers than any other method of distribution. On the other hand, a direct sales approach can be very expensive if you are covering a wide geographic area, particularly in international marketing, or if you have to train new employees. A general rule of thumb is that direct sales work best if your initial market segment is within a one-day drive of where you are. If the market is more dispersed, then you may want to consider one of three indirect sales methods.

The first indirect sales method is the use of *manufacturer's representatives*. These are independent sales people or organizations who represent several different products from different companies at the same time. They usually work on commission, which means that they only make money when they sell your product. On the positive side, representatives are much less expensive than a direct sales force, and they usually know their territory pretty well. On the negative side, most representatives carry many product lines, so there is really no way to guarantee that they will give your product the attention it needs.

The second indirect method is *national distribution*. In this case, you sell to a company at a discount. They then sell products through catalogues or by telephone, all over the United States, to resellers who sell your product directly. National distributors can give your product good exposure, easing your receivables (i.e., they are the ones who wait to get paid), keep your inventories (so you don't need as much warehouse space of your own), and advertise your product. On the downside, national distributors only push the products that are making them the most money, and if they don't pay, you are in deep trouble—quickly.

Regional distributors work in the same fashion in a smaller geographical area.

You can provide your product at wholesale prices to *retailers* who then sell your products directly to customers. These retailers come in different forms. Some are mass merchants who purchase large volumes of products in exchange for large discounts. Others are retailers who are more product-line specific, which usually means they are smaller or sell fewer products. The good news is the volume of your product purchased is high; the bad news is that they may take a long time to pay for the product and may compete with each other, causing price erosion.

To summarize, you can sell your product directly or indirectly. Each method has an upside and a downside which should be weighed carefully before you make your distribution choice. Remember, your goal is to sell as much of your product to as many people as possible with as little effort and cost as you can.

The first decision to make is whether you want to sell your product directly or indirectly. Most companies with new products test their market by first selling their products directly to their customers. You may want to try this to see if it works. If you do plan to sell directly, take the time to get sales training for your people. Browse through your local or business school library for books and tapes. Hire people with backgrounds similar to your customers' backgrounds to sell your product. For example, if your product is software for accounting and computer, hire people with accounting knowledge and teach them to sell.

If you want to sell indirectly, follow your competitors lead for distribution until you know better. Their behavior, assuming they have a significant market share, should suggest a distribution strategy to you.

To double check your choice, ask yourself if your method of distribution matches the way you want to position your product in the market. You shouldn't be selling a low-cost, standardized product at Saks Fifth Avenue any more than you should sell an expensive, high quality, limited quantity wine in a grocery chain (unless its an upscale grocery store, often described as a "specialty food shop").

Packaging

One of the last things many entrepreneurs think about is the container that will house that product. Yet your product's container can make the difference between your success or failure. The package defines your product and serves as its spokesperson, explaining what's inside and tapping the customer's perception of what he or she wants.

Name

Packaging starts with a name. I once heard a great story about a company which, trying to come up with a name for a new whiskey, set up taste tests all over the United States. In these tests, people were given four small cups of whiskey to taste. **The same whiskey was in each cup.** Even so, the tasters overwhelmingly agreed that only one of the "four" whiskeys was smooth and tasteful enough to bring to market. Their choice was totally dependent on name choice. Your product's name tells your customers what to expect, so be careful to select a name that you think is terrific before you try it out on potential customers for their reactions. I have been curious, for example, about Ford's choice of the name "Probe" for one of its recent car models. From this woman's perspective, that name conjures up visions of the gynecologist's office, not a particularly agreeable connotation.

In addition to the name, there are five important decisions that all marketers need to make relative to product packaging. Included are decisions about copy, illustration, type face, color, and container. In an excellent article in *Venture* in December, 1988, Warren Strugatch outlined each of these in some depth. For right now, the important thing to remember is that each of these packaging decisions is critical and can make the difference between someone deciding to try your product or choosing to ignore it.

Copy

Copy is made up of the words you choose to describe your product. A few well chosen words can evoke very positive associations for customers. On a recent package created for a snack manufacturer, only three key phrases were used: "No cholesterol. No preservatives. Original recipe." The absence of additives helps sell the product to health conscious consumers, while "original recipe" gives one a sense of solidness because it suggests that the company has been around for a while and is here to stay—another key consumer criteria right now.

Illustrations

We have moved into a time period when consumers obtain more information from visual modes than the written word. As a result, illustration concerns are critical. Be careful to make sure your designers are adept at fine-tuning illustrations to meet specific market purposes. When Gerbers Baby Food redid its Junior Juice line, it stopped using the traditional smiling baby photo. Instead, their new label featured a watercolor of fruits against a backdrop of a country orchard, making people think of a page from a child's picture book. In that way, they are able to sell their food to an increasingly multi-ethnic, multi-cultural consumer world.

Typeface

Typeface is the slant, thickness, style, and other characteristics of lettering. Different typefaces create very different reactions in different consumers. For example, you don't want to use strong, masculine-looking typeface if you are selling cotton lingerie. At the other extreme, you may not want to use Victorian style typeface to market a computer sturdy enough for factory floor use. There are thousands of existing typefaces or lettering types you can use on your packaging. The best way to select typeface is to get a savvy graphic artist to help you choose it.

Color

Colors can help your customers identify your product among similar products. Coffee drinkers, for instance, look for green labels when they want the decaffeinated version. Regular coffee tends to have red labels. Tea is often labelled in the same way. Colors have a significant impact on purchasing behavior. In virtually every fashion season, certain colors are "in" while others are "out." As I write, for example, metallic colors are just coming "in;" bright surfer colors are on the way "out." In marketing, you want to stay slightly ahead of your customers in your color choice, if you can afford it. The reason is that your customers perceive you as being state-of-the-art when your packaging is at the forefront of consumer tastes. That's why many large corporations change their advertising and brochures as often as they do. If you can't afford new colors every year, an acceptable default is to use "royalty" colors: blue, maroon, deep purple, etc. The reason is that royalty colors conjure up associations with the "best" or the "wealthiest," etc. Most of us want both of those attributes in our lives.

Container

Containers range from traditional to innovative types. Some offer the convenience of easy disposal, while others suggest permanence and durability. Use your customers' tastes as your guide in choosing a container. In the 1990s, however, there is one unalterable truth about containers—they should be made of recyclable material whenever possible. Why? Because the ability of a container to be recycled has become an indicator of how much a company cares about its community, how earth friendly it is.

Example: Product Requirements

Marcotte's Meat Market

Marcotte's Meat Market has decided to change its product line to meet changing customer demands for less meat, less fat, etc. The owners decided to market the store as an environmentally concerned operation. In keeping with that decision, they no longer sell red meat, concentrating their new product line on fresh fish with vegetarian accoutrements. Their packaging decisions are listed below:

New name: Marcotte's Fish Market

Copy: Always Fresh. Earth Friendly.

Illustration: All advertisement illustrations have a pen and ink sketch of the Earth in the background

Typeface: Strong and Linear

Color: Only colors used in ads are earth greens with black typeface. The green is used sparingly, only to emphasize a point in advertisements.

Container: All products are wrapped in paper. No plastic is on the premises.

Exercise 10-5

Now you try it. List below the packaging requirements for your product.

_____

_____

_____

_____

_____

_____

_____

_____

_____

_____

_____

_____

_____

_____

_____

_____

_____

_____

_____

_____

_____

_____

_____

_____

You have now thought through enough specific information to be able to spell out your product's requirements. Remember, this is where you cover features, pricing, distribution, *and* packaging.

Example: Product Requirements

Suzanna Smith's Smoked Salmon Slices

Our smoked salmon slices will be sold in one-pound boxes in the gourmet foods section of major grocery chains. The salmon will be sliced into 1/2" thick, 8" long pieces with an average of 20 slices per box. The market for the slices is inelastic, i.e., increases in prices for comparable specialty products, such as smoked trout, creamed herring, and dried orange roughy, have not historically led to a decrease in purchasing behavior.

The price of the product will be $7, wholesale; $11 retail. Discounts of 10 percent will be given for purchases of 1,000 or more pounds or for immediate cash payments. The product will be distributed nationally through GONZO Specialty Food Distributors, the largest company of its type in North America. GONZO serves every metropolitan area from Boston to Miami Beach and west to California. GONZO will organize "free sample" tables in stores close to major distribution points.

Packaging for this product is critical. Each box will be wrapped in heavy paper that has a photograph of an obviously wealthy couple eating a romantic meal with smoked salmon as the entree. The picture will be on the front of the box. Serving instructions will be written in formal script along the side of the box. The company, its address, and an "800" number will be located on the box bottom. Packaging will be made of recyclable plastic coated cardboard.

The public relations for Suzanna Smith's Smoked Salmon Slices will be the responsibility of Get Rich Quick Public Relations, Inc. Included in public relations will be press releases announcing product rollouts. The company also will undertake an intense media campaign around the theme of salmon recipes and romantic meals, using a well known celebrity as the spokesperson.

Finally, advertisements will be placed in all of the major media markets. These will be placed in key industry journals related to the specialty foods market on a quarterly basis.

Chapter Eleven

Public Relations

Public Relations

Step eleven is public relations, something every company needs. Public relations is the fine art of getting three audiences to know and love you. The first audience is made up of your customers. If customers don't know about your product, then obviously they won't buy it. The second audience is your community. Your community is important because it provides you with staff, customers, and your reputation. This is true whether you are selling to a local, regional, national, or international market. The third audience is the media. Media attention can make a company. For some reason that only psychologists attempt to understand, media attention gives instant credibility in the marketplace. Whenever I am interviewed by a reporter and later quoted in a paper or magazine, I always receive a surge of inquiries about my services.

Public relations activities are many. Choosing which activities you want to focus on to get the attention of these audiences can be difficult. When in doubt, try one activity at a time to see how it's working before you decide to try out additional public relations activities. Before you do anything in public relations, it is important to take a closer look at each of your audiences.

Community

The community is the first audience you need on your side. Without community support, no one survives. Your community verifies who you are and what business you represent. If your community says, "They're good," you'll be able to keep going. If your community says, "She lies," or, "They over-promise and under-produce," you might as well close your doors. (I refer to community as a whole here, not individuals. We all have someone who hates us. In fact, if there isn't someone out there who hates you, you probably aren't making the most of your public relations opportunities).

I've experienced the direct impact of community on companies a couple of times. With one company in particular, word got out that they didn't pay their bills. Well, you know what that does. They went out of business because no one would sell to them, and sales started to slide rapidly. They failed not because they changed their products at all; they didn't. Nor did they fail because their market size dropped; it didn't. It happened because they lost the support of their community.

You've all seen what community support does. Another example in my community is Cottage Inn Pizza restaurants. Here they are in the middle of a town where Dominos Pizza has its world headquarters, and their sales continue to grow. Why? Year after year people in Ann Arbor vote that Cottage Inn has the best pizza in town. Part of the reason is because the company is an institution with broad community support. That's where we take our parents when they're in town, and that's where we go for pizza for many community events, social gatherings, and parties.

Public relations methods that are relevant here include:

Advertising: which includes all the mechanized ways that exist which can reach the community. Advertisements can be in print, on the radio, television, video, people (t-shirts), billboards, vehicles and creative objects like balloons and banners.

Promotions: includes coupons or discounts that have a time limit.

Events: include grand openings, anniversary celebrations, and major expansions.

Philanthropy: making charitable donations back to the community.

Sponsorship of major events is also public relations. An example is Deloitte & Touche's sponsorship of the Grammy Awards.

Your Customers

Clearly, public relations is critical when it comes to customers. As I said earlier, a customer isn't a customer until he or she knows you're out there and public relations is made up of all the ways that you get that attention whether it's advertising, sales, press releases, samples, events, or anything else you can imagine.

The Media

Remember that the media makes you real. I'm always amazed at the power of the media in building the credibility of a business. Every time I'm in a newspaper or on TV, it's worth anywhere from 10 to 100 phone calls to Deloitte & Touche. My best media story is the story of

Nordstrom's out on the West Coast. Some of you media folks may re-member this.

About two years ago, *Newsweek* did a story about Nordstrom's. The theme of the article was its incredible customer service.

Nordstrom's is a clothing store with a policy of doing everything it can to keep its customers happy. I'm from Portland, Oregon, so I remember hearing stories of wedding dresses delivered in person on Sunday after-noons at the last minute and salespeople driving 100 miles to bring customers accessories or keeping the store open an extra couple of hours because someone couldn't get there before 6 p.m. That's equivalent to keeping one of your community's largest stores open after hours for one person. The *Newsweek* story was wonderful. It was about this man who showed up one day and threw a tire on the counter—he was a Nordstrom's customer, but Nordstrom's doesn't sell tires. He wanted his money back, and *they gave it to him*. Then they became national heroes in customer service thanks to *Newsweek*, and their sales grew significantly.

What helps get that kind of media attention?

Press releases. A short, specific write-up about a topic of interest helps get that attention. It needs to answer the following questions (hopefully in the first paragraph): who the release is about; what it is about; where you are talking about; why you are writing the release; when did this event take place (or when will it take place); and who is the contact. All of this information should be included in no more than five paragraphs. There are lots of books on press releases available. To get you started, an exam-ple is given below.

Media Events: These are occasions where the media is invited to some-thing like a press conference or a panel of experts on a specific and timely topic, or an important speech, etc.

Articles, letters, and speeches sent to the media also might help to estab-lish you as an expert. (Opinionated intelligent telephone calls can work here, too).

Getting All Three Audiences on Your Side

There are all sorts of activities, related to public relations, which you can do to gain a favorable reputation in your marketplace. The important thing I've found is to remember some hard learned public relations "truths."

Example: Press Release

FOR IMMEDIATE RELEASE

CONTACT: Ms. Lisa Pajot
Public Relations Director
(312) 555-7700

SEMINAR ON GROWTH FINANCING OFFERED

Houston, TX—The seminar "Financing for Growth" will be presented on Friday, March 16, 1992 from 9 a.m. to noon at the Houston Hyatt as a part of the winter seminar series for entrepreneurs and growth-minded companies. The event is sponsored by L. Willis, Inc. Cost to attend is $105 per person. To register, or for more information, call (216) 555-7700.

Topics discussed at the seminar will include:

How to tell if you need growth capital

Private Placements

Equity Investments

Employee Stock Ownership Plans

Bank Financing

BIDCOs

L. Willis, Ph.D., will present the seminar. Also featured will be a panel of experts which includes an attorney, banker, and equity expert.

L. Willis Inc. is a management consulting firm specializing in helping small to mid-sized companies in the Southwest plan for growth and locate financing.

#

Truth One: Know that everything you do is public relations—everything: from your "attitude" to your office to the voice of the person who picks up the phone to the letters you write. How you teach Sunday School is public relations. How you handle your marginal golf game is public relations. Whether you hand deliver your report to your client is public relations. Today is not too soon to take a look at yourself from the viewpoint of the community, your customers, and the media, asking yourself where you need work. And we all need work.

Truth Two: The place to start is with your receptionist or whoever it is that answers your phone. They need to sound like they love the person on the other end, whoever it is, and they need to be sincere, which means that you need to look for a real "people person" for that position. The good news is that they exist. The bad news is that it can take awhile to find them.

I have a corollary truth here. Don't use an answering machine or "voice mail" when you can have a real voice on the other end of the line. Human beings are social animals. We want to interact with people. On the surface, this might not seem like a big deal, but it is. It can be the difference between being taken seriously and being written off as a non-player in the industry. Logo, letterhead, your name, and address all come into play here as well.

Truth Three: I like advertising a lot if it is intelligently placed. Advertising can make your community, customers and the media know and like you. But be careful. Only advertise where you will really be noticed.

Truth Four: Learn how to write a press release, even if you have some else to write them for you. You should be doing press releases any time you hit a milestone—new office, new staff, new clients, awards, new products, new names.

Truth Five: Press releases are a pain in the neck and easy to forget unless you make them a part of some ongoing system like management or marketing meetings, or, if it's just you, every month sitting down to consider press release subjects.

If your company puts out a newsletter, send a copy to key journal editors. Invite editors to seminars held by your organization; they can glean articles that may never have occurred to you. Tailor news releases to specific markets.

Truth Six: Events can be powerful tools.

Cottage Inn puts on a pizza bash every school year for the freshmen at the University of Michigan, and guess who buys their pizza?

Another firm I know sponsors financial information days with key reporters from all major media in major markets. The reporters are invited for a day-long session on things like reading financial reports, what the newest estate planning laws are, etc. It is well received, and who do you think gets called for opinions when a reporter doesn't quite understand a financial planning matter?

Truth Seven: Community leadership is also an important part of public relations. It comes in many forms: Chamber of Commerce membership, volunteering for some of the non-profits out there, church association. It all adds up. People get to know you and how you operate. If you do well, it leads to public support, media coverage, and customers. Most service professionals know that more business leaders come from this than any other type of activity. You all need to know this. Beyond the altruistic reasons for helping the world to be a better place, leadership also makes good business sense.

Truth Eight: Don't be afraid of creativity. It's a big part of public relations. Your creativity is often the very thing that gets your customers' attention. Let me give you some examples: A couple of years ago I received, through an associate, a creative public relations effort of one of our competitors asking for new business. The company hired a public relations firm to write a sales letter that asked for a chance at the addressee's business. If they were truly positive their current consultant was doing a fine job, they could just toss this letter. That wasn't the creative part. The creative part was that the letter was delivered *pre-crumpled* in a tiny plastic garbage can to get attention, which it did.

Example: Public Relations Campaign

Chocolate Time, Inc.

Background: Chocolate Time, Inc. is a small company that delivers chocolate candy bars, ice cream (seasonally), and chocolate drinks to office workers located in downtown Atlanta, Georgia. The company delivers the chocolate products within twenty minutes after receiving an order by telephone or facsimile machine. The minimum order is $2 for delivery. The company has been very successful due to its concentrated public relations campaign, described below.

Campaign: Chocolate Time has a three-part public relations campaign. Regarding its customers, advertisements are placed monthly in the *Atlanta Observer* and in the Chamber of Commerce monthly newsletter *"Business to Business."* Included in each ad is a 50 percent discount coupon for a customer's first order and a 25 percent discount coupon for orders over $10. To attract the attention of both new customers and the community at large, Chocolate Time regularly participates in an annual community-wide charitable event, The Chocolate Extravaganza. All proceeds from the event go to the Atlanta Children's Shelter. Regarding the media, the company regularly sends press releases to six local newspapers, four radio stations, and three television stations. Events covered have included the company opening, the introduction of Chocolate Time's Triple Chocolate

Coated Ice Cream Sandwich, and the company's selection as Atlanta's most creative new company in 1991. Finally, the company always delivers samples of its new products to key reporters, editors, and other media representatives.

Now you try it.

Public Relations Campaign:

_____

_____

_____

_____

_____

_____

_____

_____

_____

_____

_____

_____

_____

_____

_____

_____

_____

_____

_____

_____

_____

_____

_____

CHAPTER ELEVEN

Putting It All Together

The Action Plan

You have arrived finally at the last step. Because of the many different tasks that need doing to deliver products to customers, sane marketers develop a marketing action plan. Basically, an action plan is an annotated "to do" list across a given time period (usually a year) in which you list all of the activities that need to be done to market your product successfully. Included are your environmental analysis, any surveys you do, all your market research, your sales strategy tasks related to meeting the customer's product requirements and your public relations campaign.

The easiest way to develop an action plan is to work from a simple time line similar to the one listed below. Although the estimated time for each function is fairly typical, you will need to make your own estimate given your new market knowledge.

Example: Marketing Plan Time Line

See the chart on the facing page. Then fill out your action plan, using the following blank chart.

The Budget

As is true of all life, every marketing activity has expenses. Worse, there are no simple rules you can follow. The reason for this is that marketing related costs vary widely from industry to industry and even within an industry, depending on your product. Instead, when you are unsure about how much something should cost, there are several resources you can approach for advice.

The first resource is a friendly banker. Many bankers use a book called Robert Morris Associates (RMA) Annual Statement Studies to decide how "normal" their client companies are, relative to other companies in the industry. The reason they can do that is because RMA lists all kinds of industry standards and ratios in it.

A second resource is an annual report, or a series of annual reports, for a company with a similar product. Even if it is a much bigger company than yours, you can get a sense of what your marketing costs should be relative to your other costs of doing business.

Month	1	2	3	4	5	6	7	8	9	10	11	12
TASK												
Develop Objectives	X											
Situational Analysis												
Economic Trends	X											
Industry Trends	X											
Legal Trends	X											
Socio-Cultural Trends	X											
Technology Trends	X											
Market Definition												
Define:												
Market		X	X									
Segment		X	X									
Competitive Analysis		X	X									
Decide Postioning		X	X									
Product Requirements												
Features			X	X	X							
Price			X	X	X							
Sales Strategy			X	X	X	X	X	X	X	X	X	X
Sales Begin					X							
Public Relations												
Press Releases			X	X	X	X	X	X	X	X	X	X
Advertisements			X	X	X	X	X	X	X	X	X	X
Community Events			X	X	X	X	X	X	X	X	X	X

Month	1	2	3	4	5	6	7	8	9	10	11	12
TASK												
Develop Objectives												
Situational Analysis												
Economic Trends												
Industry Trends												
Legal Trends												
Socio-Cultural Trends												
Technology Trends												
Market Definition												
Define:												
Market												
Segment												
Competitive Analysis												
Decide Postioning												
Product Requirements												
Features												
Price												
Sales Strategy												
Sales Begin												
Public Relations												
Press Releases												
Advertisements												
Community Events												

A third resource is a mentor—a solid, experienced business person who has been through it all. Preferably, this person will have been through it all in your industry.

A fourth possibility is a reputable advertising agency.

Listed below are marketing tasks that have some cost associated with them, either in terms of time or money. And, with great trepidation, let me offer you some additional parameters. If you spend less than 3 percent of your annual revenues on marketing expenses (remembering, of course, that staff time costs money) you probably aren't doing enough marketing. On the other hand, if you are spending more than 40 percent of your revenues on marketing, you've probably gone overboard. The way to tell if your budget is sufficient is to watch your sales; if they start to pick up as you try different sales, advertising, and public relations activities, then you probably are on the right track. If, after about six months, nothing is happening, something is probably wrong with your picture. You need to re-think your product, its market and your activities. With that range in mind, these are the activities that will cost time and/or money along with some estimates of costs. The real costs change significantly depending on the industry you are in and the product you are trying to sell.

Advertisements

Advertisements are another "all over the map" type of cost. A rule of thumb here is to budget for at least six ads if you can, because it takes approximately that many times for your customers to even notice your ad, and the ads should be in the same place. Ads can be as low as $40 in small, local newspapers, and go up to $32,000 or more in national newspapers and magazines. Radio commercials can run you a couple hundred to many thousands of dollars. If you can afford television commercials, you shouldn't be reading this workbook—you should hire a marketing director.

Community Events

Time: Up to a month of work for somebody. This can be split up over the course of a year. Money: Spend anywhere from several hundred to thousands of dollars, depending on the events.

S amples

There are no guidelines here. Just don't get too carried away.

All of these costs should be tracked continuously, across time (to see how much time you are spending on marketing), through your bookkeeping system. In other words, you want to list all of your costs on paper so that you can watch them constantly. It is very easy to lose control of marketing costs if you aren't careful.

Example: Annual Marketing Budget

The Malleable Handle Company

Situational Analysis: No charge. VP Marketing will do.

Competitive Analysis: No charge. VP Marketing & Sales will do.

Customer Survey: Personal interviews of 100 potential customers at $150 per interview. Total cost of interviews = $15,000, plus analysis at $5,000 gives a total of $20,000.

Sales Costs: Commissions of 30 percent will be paid to manufacturers representatives. Estimated revenues in one year with 15 manufacturing representatives = $1.5 million; total commissions paid = $450,000.

Trade Shows Expense: Five major trade shows at $3,000 to $5,000 each = $25,000.

Public Relations: Monthly retainer to Pajot Associates to cover the costs of press releases, special interest stories, and media relations: $3,000 per month, or $36,000.

Advertising: One-half page advertisement in major industry journal, four times a year at $2,500 per ad = $10,000. One full page advertisement in Track & Road's annual car of the year issue at $6,000 per ad = $6,000.

Community Events: Annual sponsorship of high school soap box derby = $3,000. United Way company match for employee donations = $10,000.

TOTAL BUDGET: $560,000, including sales expenses.

Exercise 12-2

Try estimating your marketing budget, including sales costs. Remember that there is no specific amount to spend—it's more important to make sure that you've covered all the types of tasks that need doing.

	TIME	COST	RESPONSIBILITY
Situational Analysis			
Competitive Analysis			
Customer Survey			
Sales Costs			
Trade Show Expenses			
Public Relations			
Advertising			
Community Events			
Total			

You now know all of the components of a marketing plan. If you've done the exercises, you've written all the parts. The last step is to pull all of the pieces together to make certain that they make sense and are consistent. The best way that I know to do this is just to do it. Write everything up in draft form and give it to someone familiar with marketing (who doesn't know and love you) to check for gaps or irrational optimism.

Example: Marketing Plan

To get you started, I offer you my last example. This is a marketing plan for a boy's play wear company.

L & P Play Wear

Situational Analysis

Overview

The steady growth of the U.S. economy combined with the increasing globalization of the clothing industry are positive trends for L & P Play Wear. Disposable incomes also are increasing, particularly among the double income and older households (45 years and older) that make up L & P's market. At the same time, courts are upholding suits against copyright and patent infringements, which means that there will be an increased protection of L & P's trademarked designs. Socio-economic trends are also positive. This will be discussed further in the section on L & P's market.

Market

The Size

Although L & P's products appeal to all income groups, the ultimate buyer for our products is a wealthy mother or grandmother. The socio-economic profile for both women is similar. Their household incomes are $50,000 per year or better; they value elegance and uniqueness in clothing; they enjoy shopping and appreciate having a little boy for whom they can purchase clothing. Often they are well travelled (which means that they will be spending time in the cities where L & P will be selling its products). The stores where they shop include retailers such as Saks Fifth Avenue, I. Magnin, and Nordstroms.

According to the U.S. Bureau of Census, in 1990, more than 396,000 women in America earned more than $50,000 in salaries. These women tend to be in major urban areas. Census trends suggest that the number is increasing steadily. At the same time, there are now more than 15 million married couples with joint incomes greater than $50,000. This number also is increasing. Twenty-four percent of these households have children. Approximately 37 percent of these children fall between the ages of one year and seven years. If we assume that these parents spend an average of $300 per year on their sons' play clothes (a low estimate), then the total U.S. market for L & P's products is approximately $405 million. This number does not include grandparents with incomes greater than $50,000 who may purchase clothing for their grandsons.

The International Lady Garment Worker Union's national research office suggests that the market for all boys' play clothes outfits is approximately $835 million. According to their most recent statistics for domestic production alone, 144 million boys' play clothes outfits were produced in 1989. This number does not include imported children's clothing.

Buyers for the retail stores that sell children's wear purchase clothing and accessories in three ways. Most often they go to showrooms located in major metropolitan areas. Second, they attend clothing trade shows. Three or four trade shows are held each year in major cities. Third, the buyers purchase inventory directly from sales representatives for different clothing wholesalers. Often, these representatives sell from their own city showrooms; others sell door to door.

Market Activities

In 1990, L & P Play Wear began selling play wear through two showrooms and trade shows in three cities: New York, Boston, and Atlanta. Since then we have contracted with three representatives who are unsalaried but are paid 15 percent to 20 percent of the product's wholesale price.

For the future, L & P plans to continue this sales strategy, i.e., using representatives for showrooms and minor trade shows while company principals sell products at major trade shows. Each city normally has three or four major trade shows per year.

The company also is planning to contact the following stores and catalogues to negotiate selling L & P products:

Neiman Marcus
Saks Fifth Avenue
I. Magnin
Children's Wear Digest
Wooden Soldier
Garnet Hill
Trifles

Based on a survey of places where the leading children's play wear manufacturers sell, the company has planned to expand its activities to Dallas, Los Angeles, and Chicago by 1992. In each city, the company will locate representatives who can show products in existing showrooms. In 1993, the company plans to further expand to Philadelphia, Palm Beach, Miami, Charlotte, Seattle/Portland, Kansas City, Denver, and Minneapolis.

In 1994, the company will further expand its representation to smaller cities and will perform a feasibility analysis of Asian and European markets. At this time, the company expects to expand internationally after 1994 if the feasibility study indicates that there is a strong market potential outside of the United States.

Market Activities

| April/May | Locate representatives in Dallas, Los Angeles, New York, and Chicago. |
| April 6 | Atlanta Women's and Children's Apparel Mart Show. |

April 8	Chicago Women's and Children's Apparel Mart Show.
April 14	Los Angeles Women's and Children's Apparel Mart.
May 26	Dallas Women's and Children's Apparel Mart.
June 1	Atlanta Women's and Children's Apparel Mart.
June 3	Chicago Women's and Children's Apparel Mart.
August 18	Dallas Women's and Children's Apparel Mart.
August 24	Atlanta Women's and Children's Apparel Mart.
August 25	Los Angeles Women's and Children's Apparel Mart.
August 26	Chicago Women's and Children's Apparel Mart.
October 12	Atlanta Women's and Children's Apparel Mart.
October 16	California Kid's Show, Los Angeles
October 20	Dallas Women's and Children's Apparel Mart.
October 22	New York Trade Show
October 28	Chicago Men, Women & Children's Trade Show.
November 3	Los Angeles Women's and Children's Apparel Mart.

Beyond 1992, the company plans to continue to participate in the same trade shows adding June and September shows in Miami, and August and October shows in Charlotte.

Public Relations

Regarding public relations, L & P Play Wear has three audiences. The company has planned specific public relations activities aimed directly at each group:

1. *Media, including Kids Fashions, Child, Young Fashions and Children's Business.*
    L & P will send press releases regarding each new line and product. Free samples and photos will be included with the releases.

The company also will look for opportunities to promote special stories about its product.

2. *Market Representatives*
    L & P will provide information kits for each of its marketing representatives. Included in the kits will be a description of what is new for the season, general information about L & P Play Wear, projections for upcoming lines, L & P brochures, product photos, and a product sheet including prices. Color advertisements will be placed in *Children's Business* just before major shows in August, October, March, and January.

3. *The Buying Public*
    L & P Play Wear plans to place a quarter-page color advertisement in *Child* magazine once a year. The company also opens its headquarters quarterly to the community, offering up to 40 percent off of its products.

Over time, L & P Play Wear plans to increase the size and marketing frequency of its advertisements in both *Children's Business* and *Child*, and will consider ads in *Kids Fashions* and *Young Fashions*.

Action Plan

The following chart summarizes L & P's marketing action plan for 1992. This will be repeated in 1993 and 1994 with the addition of four new trade shows in 1993 and four new representatives. Beyond 1994, the company's milestones may include development of its own manufacturing activities and a significant expansion of marketing activities into Europe and Japan.

April	Manufacture spring line samples. Send samples to representatives. Locate representatives in Chicago and Los Angeles.
May	Attend Dallas trade show. Hire Dallas representative.
June	Attend Atlanta and Chicago trade shows.
July	Place ad in *Children's Business*. Place ad in *Child*.
August	Attend Los Angeles and Chicago trade shows. Locate representative in Minneapolis.

September	Place ad in *Children's Business*.
October	Locate representative in Philadelphia, Miami, and Charlotte. Attend Atlanta, Los Angeles, New York, Dallas, and Chicago shows.
November	Locate representatives in Seattle/Portland, Kansas City, and Denver. Attend Los Angeles show.
December	Place ad in *Children's Business*.
January	Attend Los Angeles, New York, Miami, Chicago, Dallas and Charlotte shows.
February	Attend Atlanta show. Place ad in *Children's Business*.
March	Attend Los Angeles, New York, and Dallas shows.

This pattern of marketing activities will continue through 1993.

Costs

Finding Representatives

	New York	Dallas	L.A.	Chicago	Atlanta
Travel	$1,600	$1,600	$1,600	$1,200	$1,600
Stay	1.600	1,600	1,600	1,200	1,600
	$3,200	$3,200	$3,200	$2,400	$3,200

Showroom Costs

	New York	Dallas	L.A.	Chicago	Atlanta
Set Up	$ 600	$ 600	$ 600	$ 600	$ 600
Space Fee	2,800	2,800	2,800	2,800	2,800
	$3,400	$3,400	$3,400	$3,400	$3,400

Representative Costs (15 percent of sales)

New York	Dallas	L.A.	Chicago	Atlanta
$12,000	$12,000	$6,000	$6,000	$6,000

Total marketing cost for 1992: $116,600

Marketing costs per year thereafter: Assume 10% increase

Exercise 13-1

Write your marketing plan here:

Situational Analysis

_____

_____

_____

_____

_____

_____

_____

_____

_____

_____

_____

_____

_____

_____

_____

_____

_____

_____

_____

_____

_____

Market Description

_____

_____

_____

_____

_____

_____

_____

_____

_____

_____

_____

_____

_____

_____

_____

_____

_____

_____

_____

_____

_____

Competitive Analysis

_____

_____

_____

_____

_____

_____

_____

_____

_____

_____

_____

_____

_____

_____

_____

_____

_____

_____

_____

_____

_____

_____

_____

_____

_____

_____

_____

Market Position

_____

_____

_____

_____

_____

_____

_____

_____

_____

_____

_____

_____

_____

_____

_____

_____

_____

_____

_____

_____

_____

_____

_____

_____

_____

Customer Profile

Marketing Activities

_____

_____

_____

_____

_____

_____

_____

_____

_____

_____

_____

_____

_____

_____

_____

_____

_____

_____

_____

_____

_____

_____

Product Requirements

Pricing

Sales Strategy

Advertising Campaign

Public Relations

Action Plan

_____

_____

_____

_____

_____

_____

_____

_____

_____

_____

_____

_____

_____

_____

_____

_____

_____

_____

_____

_____

_____

_____

_____

_____

_____

_____

Budget

_____

_____

_____

_____

_____

_____

_____

_____

_____

_____

_____

_____

_____

_____

_____

_____

_____

_____

_____

_____

_____

_____

_____

_____

_____

_____

_____

_____

_____

Bibliography

Barabba, Vincent P., "The Market Research Encyclopedia," *Harvard Business Journal*, January-February, 1990

Committee on Small Business, U.S. Senate, *Handbook for Small Business: A Survey of Small Business Programs of the Federal Government*, Fifth edition, 1984, Senate document 98-33, Superintendent of Documents, U.S. Government Printing Office, Washington D.C. 20402.

Fuld, Leonard M., *Monitoring the Competition: Finding Out What's Really Going On Over There*, New York: John Wiley & Sons.

Kotler, Phillip, *Marketing Management: Analysis, Planning and Control*, New Jersey: Prentice-Hall, 1984.

Paley, Norton, *The Manager's Guide to Competitive Marketing Strategies*, New York: American Management Association, 1989.

INDEX

A

Acquired Immune Deficiency Syndrome, 31
Action plan, 185–210
Advertising, 36, 50, 178, 190, 191
  firms, 51
Agencies
  federal, 24–25
  government, 141
  state, 28
American Association of Public Opinion
  Research, 111
American Marketing Association, 147, 150
American Medical Association (Directory),
  145
American Telephone & Telegraph, 140
Analysis. *See* Environmental, Situational
Annual report, 187
Apple, 111
Architectural Digest, 36
Associated Press, 148
Association memberships. *See* Consumer
  (finding)
Associations, 143–144
  trade, 149–153
Audiences, 179–184
Automation, 42

B

Baby boomer(s), 36, 42, 49
BackPacker (magazine), 89
Bankruptcy, 138
Barron's, 61
Beach head, 48
Best Mailing Lists, 122
Bicycling (magazine), 89
BRS, 147
Budget, 8, 187–190
  estimating, 192

Business
  failures, 19
  manufacturing, 83–86
  service, 83–86, 136
Business Week, 18, 47, 148
Buying behavior, 17, 71, 73, 76, 77, 81

C

Campaign, sales, 50
Chamber of Commerce lists, 115, 145–146
Chief Executive Officer, 83–86
Chrysler, 49, 111
Coca-Cola, 49–50, 60
Colors, 34, 171
Community, 177–178
  events, 190, 191
Competition, 129–153
  See Information
  analysis, 151–153
  description/identification, 131–136
  finding, 140–146
  strengths, 133–135, 137, 151
    neutralizing, 137–140, 151
  weaknesses, 133–135, 137, 151
Competitive advantage, 140, 191
Consultants, 145–146
Consumer/Customer
  See Buying behavior, Demograhics,
    Interview, Survey, Trends
  behavior characteristics, 87–88
  definition, 49, 57
  characteristics choice, 78
  finding, 113–127
    association memberships, 122–124
    directories, 125, 126
    mailing list categories, 115–122
    techniques, 115–127
  loyalty, 49
  potential, 50

profile
  company, 59–60, 73–77, 81
  people, 57–58, 69–73
  selection, 95
  taste, 33–39
Contact listing, 19–20, 21–22
Context, importance, 4
Contracts, 18, 41
Cover
  letter, 95, 97
  sheet, 103, 104–105
Crain's Detroit Business, 51
Customer. *See* Consumer

D

Databases, 147–148
Demographics, 52
  See Consumer profile, Trends
Department of Natural Resources, 42
DIALOG, 147
Differentiation, 52
Directories. *See* Consumer (finding)
Displays, 33
Disposable income, 192
Distribution, 167–169
  channels, 159
  national, 168
Dow Jones News, 148
Dun and Bradstreet, 23, 148
  Million Dollar Directory, 115

E

Economic
  indicators, 18–19
  predictors, 22
Education, 52, 71, 73
Employment range, 71, 73
Environment
  economic, 17, 18–23
  legal, 17, 23, 24–28, 42, 43
  social/cultural, 17, 31–39, 42, 44
  technological, 17, 39–44
Environmental
  analysis, 17, 187
  issues, 42
Environmental Protection Agency, 24, 42
Environmentalists, 4, 32
Esquire (magazine), 36
Ethnicity. *See* Race

F

Feedback, 107, 113–127, 167
  See Consumer (finding), interview
  validity, 125, 127

Finances, 8
Focus groups, 107–110
  See Interview
  letter, 109
  questions, 108, 110
  rules, 108
Food and Drug Administration, 25
Forbes, 61, 148
Fortune (magazine), 18, 39, 61, 148
  500 companies, 41, 59, 66–67
Frost and Sullivan, 23

G

Gerbers, 170
Gross Domestic Product, 18, 41

H

Harris (Louis) Poll, 32
Heads of Households, 121
Heinz Corporation, 48
Hot Rod Magazine, 115

I

Impact chart, 27
Inc. Magazine, 51
Income
  personal, 18
  psychic, 32
  range, 52, 70, 73
Industrial Statistics Yearbook, 149
Industry
  Forecasts, 149
  hazardous waste, 141
  medical, 141
  overview, 19–20
  reports, 148–149
Inflation rate, 18, 41
Information gathering, 142–145
International Business Machines, 39, 141–142
International Lady Garment Worker's
  Union, 193
International Trade Administration, 25
Interview
  See Cover, Feedback, Focus group,
    Interview
  mail, 93
    advantages/disadvantages, 93, 95–103
  personal, 93, 107
    advantages/disadvantages, 94–95
  professionals, 111
  telephone, 93, 103–107
    advantages/disadvantages, 94
  questionnaires, 103
  refusals, 105–106

K

Kiplinger Newsletter, 23
K Mart, 160

L

Legal Exchange Information Service, 147, 148
Licensing, restrictions, 24
Lifestyle, 52
Little, Arthur D. Co., 23

M

Machinery, 8
Magazines, 35–36, 144
Magnin, I., 193
Mailing lists. *See* Consumer (finding)
Manufacuring, computer-aided, 42
Market
  See Penetration, Positioning
  activities, 194–195
  age, 60, 63–64, 68
  attributes, 60–69, 159–160
    example, 66–69
  clique(s), 61, 65, 69
  definition, 55–78
    tuning, 79–90
  diversity, 61, 64, 68
  growth rate, 60, 63, 68
  information, sources, 62
  matrix, 136–137
  niche, 47–48
    advantages/disadvantages, 48–50
    identification, 51
  penetrability, 61, 66, 69
  seasonality, 61, 65, 69
  segments, 82–86
    verification, 87
  sensitivity, 61, 64–65, 68
  size, 60, 62–63, 67, 193–194
  target, 80
  tastes, 160
  technology, 61, 66, 69
Marketing
  See Market, Objective
  analysis, 3
  definition, 3
  niche, 88, 89
    verification, 89–90
  segment, 89
  target, 88–89
Media, 178–179
Men's Health (magazine), 89
Merrill Lynch, 148
Morris (Robert) Associates, 187
Motorola, 39
MTV, 50–51

N

Naisbitt, John, 32
National Association of Manufacturers, 149
National Bureau of Standards, 25
Newspaper Exchange Information Service, 147
Newspapers, 144
New York Times, 32, 37, 61, 147
Niche. *See* Market, Marketing
Nordstroms, 193

O

Objective, 4–8
  accomplishing, 7
  marketing, 3, 9–13
    purpose, 9
  results, 11
Omni (magazine), 36
On-line Retrieval of Bibliographic
  Information
Organic Farming and Gardening, 89

P

Packaging, 33, 50, 169–174
  See Colors
  container, 171
  copy, 170
  illustrations, 170
  name, 169–170
  typeface, 171
Paine Webber, 148
Patent and Trademark Office, 25
Penetration, 48
  See Market
Personality traits, 58
Philanthropy, 178
Popcorn, Faith, 32
Positioning, 45, 155–174
  company, 157
  criteria, 158–161
  market, 157, 158
  product, 157
  quality, 159
  threats, 141
Predicast Forecasts, 149
Press releases, 179
Pricing, 164–167
  sensitivity, 165
Product
  application, 158, 159
  approach, 3
  awareness, 11, 12
  costs, 164, 166
  features, 163–164
    intangible, 161

tangible, 161
generic, 48
image, 11, 12
line, 75, 77
qualifications, 11, 13
requirements, 161
resistance, 11, 12
strengths/weaknesses, 133–135
type, 52
use, 52
Profile, customer. *See* Consumer
Profit, corporate, 18
Profitability, 75, 81
Promotions, 178
Public relations, 175–184, 191, 195–196
Purchasing process, 76, 77, 81

Q

Questionnaire. *See* Survey

R

Race, 31–32, 52, 70, 72
Recycling, 41, 42
Regulations, 24, 26
city, 28
government, 41
Research, 33–38, 91–111
See Focus group, Interview
market, 81
organizations, 111
Research & Development
expenditure(s), 74, 76, 77, 81
Revenues, 57, 59, 74–75, 81
Rodale Press, 89
Runner's World (magazine), 89

S

Saks Fifth Avenue, 193
Samples, 191–197
SDC, 147
Sears, 160
Securities and Exchange Commission, 146
Segment
See Market, Marketing
characteristics, 51–54
Selective Discrimination of Information, 147
Service, 136, 159
Situational analysis, 3, 4, 16–44, 191–192
definition, 17
example, 41–44
Sloan (Alfred), Foundation, 39
Sony, 60
Sponsorship, 178

Standard & Poor's, 148
Standard Industry Classification, 75, 81
Success, measurement, 6
Survey
See Consumer, Information, Interview,
Trends
customer, 49, 93–107
example, 98–101
question
closed-ended, 96
value, 101–102
questionnaire, 96
pretest, 101–102

T

Technology Futures, 23
Television, 36–37
Time limit, 6
Trends
business, 34
cultural/consumer, 37
demographic, 31–32, 37
economic, 23, 41, 43
industry, 21, 23
information organizations, 23
market, 41
national, 35
technology, 40
tracking, 4

U

Unemployment rate, 18, 41
United Press International, 148
U.S. Bureau of Census, 31, 41, 146, 193
U.S. Department of Commerce, 24, 25
Annual Outlook on U.S. Industries, 61
Bureau of Economic Analysis, 18
Business Conditions Digest, 23
Current Industrial Reports, 146
U.S. Industrial Outlook, 149
U.S. Small Business Administration, 24
Utne Reader, 36

V

Video cassette recorder, 39
Vogue (magazine), 36

W

Wall Street Journal, 18, 61, 148

Y

Yellow pages, 144

About the Author

Dr. Geraldine Larkin is Manager of the Emerging Businesses Department at Deloitte & Touche in Ann Arbor, Michigan where she provides marketing and strategic planning services to hundreds of entrepreneurial companies. She formerly directed the Michigan Department of Commerce's Office for New Enterprise Services, working with high technology companies throughout Michigan on marketing, business and financial planning, and is the co-founder of the Michigan Women's Foundation. In 1980, Dr. Larkin joined the C.S. Mott Foundation as a program officer for economic development. Dr. Larkin received her B.S. from Barnard College and holds a Ph.D. in policy analysis from Portland State University in Oregon.